GREATER
SARASOTA
from shorelines to skylines

GREATER
SARASOTA
from shorelines to skylines

published by
The Greater Sarasota Chamber of Commerce

First Published in the United States of America, in 2007
The Greater Sarasota Chamber of Commerce
1945 Fruitville Road, Sarasota, FL 34236
www.sarasotachamber.com

ISBN 978-0-9800032-0-8
LCCN 2007938130
© 2007 by The Greater Sarasota Chamber of Commerce

Printed in Sarasota, Florida, United States of America
Edited by Mark Cornish
Designed by 2COMMUNIQUÉ / www.2communique.com
Printed in Sarasota by Serbin Printing

contents

fast facts

POPULATION

City of Sarasota—55,364 (Est. 2006) Founded 1885. Incorporated 1905

Sarasota County—369,535 (Est. 2006) Established 1921

Manatee County—313,298 (Est. 2006) Established 1855

LAND AREA

City of Sarasota—25.9 sq. miles

Sarasota County—573 sq. miles

Manatee County—741 sq. miles

MILES OF GULF COAST

Sarasota County—35 miles

Manatee County—27 miles

COUNTY SEATS

Sarasota County—City of Sarasota

Manatee County—City of Bradenton

MEDIAN AGE (2004)

Sarasota County—51.7

Manatee County—42.8

PER CAPITA INCOME

(2004)

Sarasota County— $42,933

Manatee County—$32,837

AVERAGE HOUSEHOLD (2000 CENSUS)

Sarasota—2.13

Manatee—2.29

AVERAGE FAMILY SIZE

(2000 census)

Sarasota—2.61

Manatee—2.78

EMPLOYMENT COMPOSITION (2005)

For Manatee County, the following figures are for 2006 from www.labormarketinfo.com and then under "ES202"

	Sarasota County	Manatee County
Agriculture	0.2%	4.3%
Construction	11.0%	9.6%
Manufacturing	5.5%	7.9%
Transportation, Warehousing and Utilities	2.0%	4.3%
Wholesale	2.8%	2.9%
Retail	14.1%	12.5%
Services	49.0%	79.6%
Finance, Real Estate and Insurance	6.8%	9.6%
Other Services	4.3%	2.6%
Government	4.2%	4.8%

MARKET DATA

	Sarasota County	Manatee County
Unemployment Rate	3.0%	3.7% (June 07)
Number of Corporate Headquarters	40	18
Number of Businesses	14,996	11,103 est.*
Gross Metropolitan Product	$25.2 billion	$25.2 billion**
Job Growth Rate	21.65%	18.64%
New Residents Annually (2005)	35,101	24,384

*This figure varies as there is not an occupational license required for all businesses in the county. An estimate would be 11,103 from Decision Data Resources.

**For 2005. Manatee County figure is the same as Sarasota County; data available only for the MSA (Bradenton-Sarasota-Venice)

INCORPORATED CITIES & TOWNS

Sarasota County—Sarasota, North Port, Venice, Longboat Key

Manatee County—Bradenton, Palmetto, Anna Maria, Longboat Key, Bradenton Beach, Holmes Beach

AVERAGE HOUSE COST

(median sales price 2007)

$294,200

TOTAL RETAIL SALES

$9.8 billion

AVERAGE TEMPERATURES

	High	Low
January	71	49
July	91	73

AVERAGE ANNUAL RAIN DAYS
107

BEST BEACH
Crescent Beach, Siesta Key

TAMPA BAY AREA
12th largest media market in the U.S.

Workforce—1.9 million

Number of businesses—87,871

Unemployment rate—2.96%

Per capita income—$27,783

Gross regional product—$76 billion

Job growth rate—4.8%

Number of jobs created—186 daily

New residents annually—3,000

- Sarasota County lies on Sarasota Bay on the West Coast of Florida, Latitude 27.3º Longitude 82.5º.

- *CNN/Money Magazine* chose Sarasota as America's Best Small City and one of the nation's top eight "Places to Retire Young" in 2007.

- In 2007, *Inc. Magazine* ranked Sarasota-Bradenton-Venice No. 8 on a list of 393 "boomtowns," and No. 3 among mid-size cities.

- Also in 2007, *Forbes* placed the Sarasota-Bradenton-Venice MSA at No. 11 on the Top 25 Best Cities Jobs list, or the third best in Florida, one step above Tampa. When it comes to unemployment and job growth rates, the Sarasota MSA ranked the third best in the country.

- Sarasota and Bradenton were among the 100 cities cited by Relocate-America.com in 2007 as the best places to live in the U.S., based on people, neighborhoods, the beauty of the area, schools, activities, economic health, environmental health, crime, employment and housing data.

- According to the *Expansion Management* magazine and the National Policy Research Council, Sarasota-Bradenton ranks in the Top 20 Large Metros for business recruitment and attraction (out of 362 nationwide).

- In 2007, Sarasota-Bradenton was named the second best market to grow a small business by *BizJournal*.

- Sarasota has a designated Enterprise Zone east of U.S. 41 from the northern part of the city to parts of downtown. Businesses located within the zone are eligible for various tax incentives.

- There are nine hospitals in Sarasota and Manatee Counties.

- In 2006, for the third consecutive year, *US News & World Report* listed Sarasota Memorial Health Care System among the top 50 hospitals in six specialties in its prestigious "America's Best Hospitals" issue.

- Sarasota County School District was ranked among the top 17% of 2,800 school districts *Expansion Management* magazine surveyed in the U.S.

- The Sarasota-Manatee area has nine colleges and universities.

- In 2007 for the second year in a row, New College, Florida's honor college, was ranked No. 1 among "Best Value Public Colleges" in the United States by the *Princeton Review*.

- *Travel & Leisure Golf* is also on the Gulf Coast bandwagon, naming the Founders Club east of I-75 in Sarasota and Concessions in Lakewood Ranch among America's Top 100 Golf Course Communities. The publication awards the "Top 100" designation to communities that best combine superb golf with high quality homes and facilities, location and wealth of lifestyle opportunities.

- Sarasota County was named a winner of the National Civic League's All-American City Award in 2006.

- The City of Sarasota has 6 sister cities in Scotland, France, Israel, Russia, Italy and Canada with whom it conducts cultural and business exchange programs. Bradenton has a sister city in Spain.

introduction

THE CITY OF SARASOTA HAD A LOT TO BE PROUD of when it celebrated its 100-year anniversary in 2002. Long known as the cultural capital of Florida, its abundance of theaters, museums and other distinguished art institutions attracts tourists and year-round residents from all over the world. At the same time, Sarasota could point to educational institutions with international reputations, a health care system ranked among the top in the nation, superior sports and recreational facilities, and a lifestyle that is second to none.

Blessed with extraordinary physical beauty, Sarasota has often been called a tropical paradise; and with good reason. The world-renowned white sand beaches lining the coast and the barrier islands are great for walking, getting a tan and watching spectacular sunsets. A balmy climate ensures beautiful tree-lined streets and avenues, and parks, gardens and neighborhoods blossoming with lush, greenery and colorful flowers. A wide variety of residential communities throughout the county makes life a pleasure for families and retirees.

It all adds up to a vibrant, dynamic community. Thus, it has come as no surprise that the years since the centennial have brought continued growth and expansion, which has spread into every part of the surrounding county and beyond to Manatee County in the north and Charlotte County to the south.

The city of Sarasota has seen upscale high-rise condos and hotels mushroom in the downtown area, and surrounding neighborhoods revitalize with new retail stores, art galleries and restaurants. Further construction, including a billion dollar mixed-use development on the bay, is in the works. At the same time, new and existing communities throughout Sarasota County continue to grow, adding residential areas among golf courses, shopping areas, office and business parks and entertainment venues.

Tourism continues to fuel our economy. Visitors frequently fall in love with the area and return for longer stays. A few days or week-long vacation leads to a month or half year sojourn and, ultimately, to a permanent residence. But while the area continues to be a haven for retirees, the population is also getting younger each year with newcomers putting down roots. In 2007, the median age in Sarasota County was 51.7 years and 42.5 in Manatee County.

As younger, affluent and well-educated residents move to the area, they affect every-thing from real estate, building development, retail venues and sports and entertainment facilities. In addition, they make possible a wide variety of traditional and new employ-ment opportunities. In fact, when it comes to unemployment and job growth rates, the Sarasota-Manatee-Venice MSA is ranked the third best in the United States.

A younger, highly educated workforce, along with financial incentives on the part of state, county and city, and progressive local business leadership, has made the area a magnet for high-tech manufacturers and companies with international reach. Sarasota County is home to nearly 40 corporate headquarters, a number that will continue to grow in the coming years. The area consistently ranks among the top large metros in the nation for business recruitment and attraction.

At the same time, existing businesses are expanding, and entrepreneurs are creating new startups in record numbers. In 2007, Sarasota-Bradenton was named the second best market to grow a small business by *BizJournal*.

These trends will continue. As part of the Florida High Tech Corridor, the Sarasota-Manatee area will continue to attract cutting edge businesses and manufacturing companies. Ongoing business expansion and development add up to a bright future for the region.

One of the major factors contributing to Sarasota's ongoing success story is the ability to offer a magnificent quality of life to all comers. Splendid weather, miles of beautiful beaches and a wide variety of employment opportunities draw people to our area from around the nation and the world. In addition, an outstanding public and private school system, a number of impressive colleges and universities, top-notch hospitals, high quality arts organizations and superior recreational facilities all make it easy to see why we are so appealing.

Indeed, with its current population of 360,000 projected to swell to 532,000 over the next 25 years, the county will continue on its trajectory toward excellence. As a mecca for tourists, business owners, and individuals and families seeking to make a wonderful life for themselves, Sarasota is poised to become one of the greatest 21st century destinations.

history &
heritage

history

DURING THE 16TH CENTURY, THE SPANISH conquistadors came to Florida seeking gold and the fountain of youth. They didn't find what they were looking for, but they were impressed by the beauty of the landscape, the scenic bays filled with a variety of fish, the lush forests populated by Indians and all kinds of game, and the balmy climate.

The encounters with the thriving population of aboriginal Indian tribes—

the Tocobagas and the Calusas—did not go well for either side. Ponce de Leon sailed into Charlotte Harbor just south of Sarasota and died there after being wounded in a fierce Indian attack. Hernando de Soto, made landfall in 1539 on what is now Longboat Key, one of the barrier islands of Sarasota Bay, before headquartering on the Manatee River just to the north. He burned villages and tortured the natives for information about gold and eventually concluded that there was none to be found. Three years later he died while exploring the southern United States.

There is a story about a love affair between an Indian Chief and de Soto's daughter Sara, and many like to think that it was Sara De Soto who bequeathed her name to the town and area. It's a lovely tale, but unfortunately the stuff of legend, since the Spanish explorer never had a daughter.

Seminole Indian Chief Holata Micco, aka. Billy Bowlegs.

There have been other explanations for the name. Some believe that it came from the Seminole Indian trading post known as Saraxola. Others have suggested that it is a corruption of Spanish phrases, ranging from "sorao sota" (place of dancing) to "zarsosa" (briery) and "sota" (thicket or grove), a reference to the dense vegetation the earliest arrivals encountered.

Whatever the case, the name Sarazota or Porte Sarasote, and later Sara Sota, became associated with the bay on maps and in documents, and the name stuck. By 1839, the official name for the area was Sarasota.

AFTER THE CONQUISTADORS

For more than two centuries, the bay became the outpost for Spanish fishermen from Cuba and the Caribbean islands. They built fish camps, or ranchos, along the shores during the winter months and sent their catch — mullet, pompano, carp and trout — back to markets in Havana. They also cultivated fields and gardens and planted orange trees brought from their distant homes that would become one of the symbols of the future Sunshine State.

For the Indians, the encounters with the white men marked a clash of cultures that spelled their doom. Their numbers declined, decimated by warfare, slavery, disease and epidemics. In fact, the Indians most associated with Florida, the Seminoles, were recent arrivals, too, moving into the state during the mid 1700s and they became hired laborers and companions to the wintering fishermen.

Although Florida, as a colony, changed to British ownership and reverted to Spain, it had little impact on the lives of the Spanish fishermen, who along with their compadres in Tampa Bay and to the south in Charlotte Harbor, formed a Gulf Coast community.

THE 1800s

In 1821, Spain ceded Florida to the United States. Congress divided the territory into counties. Sarasota was first part of Hillsborough County, and when that was subdivided in 1856, it ended up in Manatee County. It wasn't until 1921 that Sarasota became its own county.

For much of the 19th century, Florida remained a frontier territory. As cowboys, planters and tradesmen flocked to the region, there were two brutal wars with the Seminoles.

The first white settler in the Sarasota area arrived in 1842; Florida achieved statehood in 1845. William Whitaker, a veteran of the Second Seminole War, went into the cattle business and purchased a homestead covering 145 acres. Other families soon joined. Life was hard and primitive. There were neither roads nor bridges. Supplies and news from the outside world came by schooner from Tampa. Mosquitoes and sand fleas made the outdoors all but unbearable during the rainy summer months.

Following the Civil War, the area attracted a number of pioneers. More than a hundred families moved to the region. They included the Knights and the Webbs, and Charles Abbe who settled at Phillippi Creek. He soon became the largest landowner in the area, acquiring 400 acres, and opened a general store. He also petitioned the government for a post office. When the request was approved in 1878, Abbe became the first postmaster of the new community of Sara Sota.

The 1880s brought land speculation and the arrival of Scottish colonists. Lured by the Florida Mortgage & Investment Company's promise of 40 acre estates, 23 families crossed the Atlantic by steamboat. They were bitterly disappointed. Their land turned out to be in the backwoods some six to eight miles from shore. A freezing winter didn't help, and most of the colonists returned to Scotland after only three months.

But a few hardy souls remained. A.C. Acton, the local manager of the Florida Mortgage & Investment Company put up a wharf and a two-story rooming house at Five Points, the intersection of Main, First and Pineapple streets. Another colonist, Dr. Thomas Wallace, constructed a house and opened a clinic on the north side of Main Street. Across the street, two of William Whitaker's sons added a general store.

With the arrival of John Hamilton Gillespie, the son of the part owner of the Florida Mortgage & Investment Company, things began to take off. Gillespie built a three-story, 30-room hotel on the waterfront and named it the De Soto. Wooden sidewalks were laid along Main Street from Five Points to the wharf. A golf enthusiast, Gillespie also cleared the woods and created the first practice golf course in Florida, perhaps in the U.S., comprising a long fairway and two greens.

By 1887, Sara Sota may still have been a village, but it had a real downtown and was bustling with workmen and new arrivals. More than two hundred attended the festivities when Gillespie's De Soto hotel opened with a grand ball that February.

With the outbreak of the Spanish-American War in 1898, prosperity came to the Gulf Coast fisheries and cattle trade. They sent their supplies to the American soldiers staged in Tampa, the embarkation port for Cuba. The following year, the first telephone line premiered between Bradenton and the Sarasota post office, now located on the corner of Main and Pineapple. Although the area had a population of only 600, the town met the new century with considerable optimism.

THE EARLY 1900s

As Florida entered the 20th century, Sarasota was swept along in the race to modernize. The Gulf Coast Telephone Company signed up its first subscribers. The Seaboard Air Line Railway that went from Tampa to Naples had a stop in Sarasota. The first bridge across the Manatee River was built and the area slowly grew.

What really put Sarasota and environs on the map was the visit of Mrs. Potter Palmer in 1910. A wealthy Chicago society woman known for her business sense, she fell in love with the area. Soon, she and her family invested heavily in property, ultimately owning more than a quarter of the land in what is now Sarasota County. She established a model cattle ranch, now an upscale golf course community, created an experimental farm on Bee Ridge Road, and built a showplace estate in Osprey. Her influence and dedication to the area, more

Five Points, ca. 1925. Construction underway on the First Bank and Trust Company which would later become the Palmer Bank.

SARASOTA MEMORIAL HEALTHCARE FOUNDATION, INC.

ESTABLISHED 1976 **www.smhf.org**

Advancing Healthcare Through Philanthropy For More Than Three Decades

This is a story of what can happen when dedicated people harness private efforts for the public good.

In the 1970s, with Sarasota's population expanding and Sarasota Memorial Hospital struggling to keep pace with rapid developments in technology to support the advances in patient care nationwide, the need for a separate organization to solicit the support of citizens for the hospital was apparent.

As one of the Foundation's founders, Ted Watson said, "We were all of the same mind—that the hospital was an important institution and healthcare was close to everyone's heart. It was only natural to create the Foundation and focus the community on the hospital."

And so, on February 25, 1976, Sarasota Memorial Hospital Foundation, Inc. was established as an independent, not-for-profit corporation. Its charter is broad; it may receive gifts, grants and bequests for restricted or unrestricted purposes. It may aid any not-for-profit healthcare organization in the county and it may expend funds for equipment, clinical studies, research training, community education programs, and now, capital improvements.

As the Foundation's mission became known, support from the community demonstrated that the people of Sarasota truly valued the community's overall healthcare needs and understood the importance of the outstanding public hospital that would make its services available to all its residents. And that those services would be among the nation's finest.

Making an Impact

The Foundation's first grant helped purchase a system of bedside cardiac monitoring equipment. It was soon followed by the purchase of a CAT scanner that allowed for quick, safe and painless diagnosis. In April 1983, a gift funded the opening of the Open Heart Surgery Center, the foundation of a cardiac program that repeatedly ranks among the nation's 50 best hospitals.

In the late '80's, bequests resulted in the construction of the Cape Ambulatory Surgery Center, and the purchase of

Above: Charles R. (Chick) Estill, Founding Foundation President & CEO, and Harlow S. (Red) Heneman, Chairman of the Board, display the Sarasota Memorial Hospital Foundation Medallion in 1976

Right from top, Maternal-Neonatal Intensive Care Transport Unit. The da Vinci S™ Surgical System®

Sarasota's first MRI, technology that provided radiologists images of unprecedented clarity.

As the Foundation's reputation grew, so did the community's generosity. It received gifts to aid in building and endowing the Jo Mills Reis Care Center, to create the Meckler Admission Center; to establish the first endowed chair and professorship at the University of South Florida College of Nursing; and to provide scholarships for continuing education so the hospital could continue to meet the demand for highly skilled medical staff.

Other grants made possible the purchase of specialized brain-surgery equipment and a research affiliation with

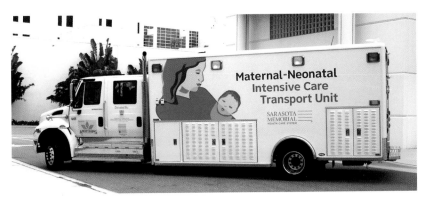

rapidly changing technology, the Healthcare Foundation is similarly presented with great challenges—and great opportunities—in its efforts to continue to support the hospital's mission and the community's healthcare.

The Sum of its People

Grants totaling more than $32 million have been provided since the Foundation's establishment in 1976. With more than $37 million in assets and growing, it stands ready to assure the community that not only will Sarasota Memorial Health Care System continue to be one of the best medical centers in the country—other local not-for-profit healthcare organizations will benefit as well.

The Foundation has been most fortunate for the foresight of its trustees and the financial support of the community in furthering its mission.

Sarasota Memorial Healthcare Foundation, Inc. has never lost sight of the fact that it is the sum of its people—of the dedicated, caring individuals who have gone before and those who continue to believe in quality healthcare for all in our community. It has been a remarkable story of caring individuals who have humanized a county hospital through private philanthropy—an extraordinary journey of VOLUNTARY ACTION FOR THE PUBLIC GOOD.

Harvard Medical School to study Parkinson's and other neurodegenerative diseases. These helped lead to the establishment of Sarasota Memorial's Neuroscience Center of Excellence.

Recently, the Foundation has provided funding for the new and expanded Emergency Care Center (ECC), the area's first digital mammography equipment, a Maternal-Neonatal Intensive Care Transport Unit, a surgical navigation system for knee and hip replacement, and most recently, the new da Vinci S robot that assists surgeons in performing minimally invasive heart and cancer surgeries.

Meeting Community Needs

Sarasota Memorial Health Care System has evolved into one of the premiere healthcare centers in the United States, recognized in study after study as a leader in heart care and heart surgery, cancer, digestive disorders, gynecology, orthopedics and respiratory disorders. Today, no other hospital in the region offers this range of services, technology and equipment. It is eloquent testimony to the wisdom, foresight and hard work of the Foundation's founders and its subsequent leaders who have made this and much more possible.

Furthering the Mission

As Sarasota Memorial Health Care System strives to continue providing nationally recognized healthcare services in the face of increased competition, declining reimbursements and

Bertha Potter Palmer (top) who first arrived in Sarasota in 1910; the pergola at Mrs Palmer's estate at Historic Spanish Point.

than anyone else, gave Sarasota a cache of wealth and aristocracy, and attracted a wave of investors to make it a fashionable winter resort.

With the advent of tourism, the area's image changed from a quaint fishing village to a modern day city. Hotels, motels and attractions sprung up to welcome the Tin Can Tourist, who brought money to the economy. In 1915, Sarasota officially incorporated as a city.

At the same time, the cattle and citrus industries flourished. The fact that there are two growing seasons in Florida allowed agriculture to become a major industry as well. The "celery fields" east of I-75, now providing runoff areas during major rainfall, go back to the time when tomatoes and celery first became major crops.

THE ROARING TWENTIES

The real estate boom that hit Florida like a hurricane in the 1920s sent waves of prosperity to Sarasota. The area population increased from 3,000 to 15,000 in six years. Buildings shot up like mushrooms. Many of them, such as the Edwards Theatre, now home of the Sarasota Opera, and the Francis Carlton Apartments on Palm Avenue, still stand today.

Along with the boom came a number of firsts whose influence continues into our day. In 1921, Sarasota became its own county, breaking off from Manatee County. The new county line was just a dirt road then. Now University Park Parkway is a six-lane thoroughfare.

Big league baseball discovered the benefits of warm weather. The New York Giants first made the area their headquarters for spring training in 1926. Since then, a number of major league teams have followed their lead. Currently, the Pittsburgh Pirates play in Bradenton, while the Cincinnati Reds compete at Ed Smith Stadium in Sarasota.

The first Mennonite family came to Sarasota in 1925 to work on the celery farms. As others joined, a sizeable Mennonite community developed. As a result, the area can claim many Amish-style restaurants whose popular dishes have lines waiting to be seated during the tourist season.

But the most prominent development occurred in 1927 when John Ringling decided to move the winter quarters of the Ringling Brothers, Barnum and Bailey

Air Force trainees at the Sarasota-Bradenton Air Base, ca. early 1940s.

Circus—The Greatest Show on Earth—to Sarasota. Ringling and his wife Mabel had been coming to Sarasota since 1912. A developer, as well as a circus magnate, he built the first causeway to Lido Key, hoping to develop the islands. He built a palatial home and an art museum on a large estate on the water, and later endowed a school for the arts, which has grown into an elite institution.

Ringling's arrival and influence could not have come at a better time. By the mid-twenties, the real estate boom had gone bust throughout Florida, anticipating the coming of the Great Depression by several years, but in Sarasota it was not felt as deeply because the circus coming to town brought with it a virtual army of workers, animal trainers and performers, providing a boost to the local economy.

THE 1930s AND 40s

The Great Depression pulled the economic rug out from under Sarasota's high life. In the 1930s, under the New Deal, various National Recovery organizations arrived. The Work Projects Administration (WPA) made possible the creation of Myakka State Park on land largely donated by the Palmer family. It also built a 37-acre Bayfront Park on Sarasota Bay located just a block from downtown. Additional projects included the Sarasota Municipal Auditorium, a large hangar-like structure on the North Tamiami Trail, and the Lido Beach Pavilion.

During the Second World War, Florida's balmy weather and open spaces made the state an appealing training ground for the Air Force. Of the 40 training bases and schools that sprung up throughout the state, two were in Sarasota County.

As a result, a new airport was built in joint cooperation between Manatee and Sarasota Counties, and an airfield was constructed in Venice. By 1942, 6,000 military men were stationed there. After the war, both air bases were deactivated and placed under civilian control.

The war years also brought relief from the Depression. Military personnel and their various support services brought a new influx of people. Housing facilities that had been lying half empty were suddenly filled to capacity. Florida once again became a destination. By the end of the war decade, Florida's population had nearly doubled, while Sarasota's population had increased by 85 percent.

In 1947, a delegation from Sarasota successfully introduced a measure in the State House of Representatives to create a city manager form of municipal government. Since then, the city has been governed by a board of commissioners, which selects a city manager and rotates the mayorship among its ranks.

THE 1950s AND 60s

Post-war prosperity and air-conditioning ensured that Florida and Sarasota would thrive as never before. People flocked to the Sunshine State to spend winters and retirement away from the cold northern climate. Snowbirds and retirees infused the local economy with money.

SARASOTA YACHT CLUB

ESTABLISHED 1926 **www.sarasotayachtclub.org**

Scenically located in a sheltered cove on one of the keys in Sarasota Bay, the Sarasota Yacht Club combines a rich history with the most up-to-date modern facilities. Comfortable and inviting, it is the perfect home away from home for its members. The club provides the perfect opportunity to entertain guests, make new friends, improve boating skills, swim and fish, or embark on an adventuresome cruise. Its members include successful business people and professionals from all parts of the U.S. and Europe with reciprocal privileges at hundreds of clubs around the world.

First organized in 1907, the Sarasota Yacht Club was incorporated in 1926 as one of the original members of the Florida Council of Yacht Clubs. For some time, it made its home on Siesta Key and later on Gulfstream Avenue in downtown Sarasota before finally settling on land donated and deeded on Coon Key in 1940. During World War II, the United States government leased the club property for use as an Air Force Crash Boat Rescue Base. When the club regained control of the property, the two barrack buildings from the war served as a clubhouse for many years; a new clubhouse was built in 1958. Since then the SYC has undergone a number of expansions, additions and renovations, the most recent in 2002, which extended and modernized the dock area.

Whether you're a yachting devotee or merely want to enjoy the benefits of a private social club, the Sarasota Yacht Club offers outstanding services and facilities.

With easy deep water access to both the Intracoastal Waterway and the Gulf of Mexico, the marina's docks can accommodate boats up to 100 feet length overall (LOA) and 10 feet draft. The 108 slips, available to members and visiting boaters, are equipped with new electrical pedestals that have meters and outlets for cable television and telephone. Other recent improvements include security lighting, new fuel and fire lines, additional transformers and a pump-out station. There are full-time dock-master services, free Wi-Fi access, discounted fuel prices for members and a convenient launch ramp for trailer boats.

A friendly, inviting atmosphere pervades the Club, making it a popular venue for relaxation and entertainment. The swimming pool offers members and visiting boaters the opportunity for a refreshing dip. Twenty-four-hour bath and shower facilities are also available.

Dining can be formal or just-in-from-the boat casual. The Club offers luncheons and dinners six days a week in the Main Dining Room and informal lunch in the Porthole Bar & Grille or on the veranda next to the swimming pool. The large dining room that can seat up to 500 guests, along with two bars and various smaller rooms for private functions, make the Sarasota Yacht Club a great place for banquets, small party events and important meetings.

There are numerous yachting activities throughout the year, including luncheon day cruises to local waterfront restaurants and weekend trips to other yacht clubs within a day's run. An annual extended cruise visits places as far away as Key West, the Bahamas or Charleston, North Carolina. The Sarasota Yacht Club Invitational Regatta has become a popular event that promotes sailing, and the spectacular Lighting of the Fleet just before Christmas, in which boats throughout the marina display brightly colored lights, is a perennial favorite.

Social events dominate the calendar throughout the season. Formal functions like the Commodore's Ball vie with once-a-month theme parties, including luaus and lobster feasts. Other important celebrations include the Change of Watch, when the new Commodore and Bridge Officers are introduced in October, and the Candle Light Dinner and New Years Eve Celebration in December.

With its wide range of activities and superior modern amenities, the Sarasota Yacht Club has become the premiere yacht club in the Sarasota area, a favorite port of call for maritime enthusiasts from all over the world.

An explosion of new residential and municipal construction led to the development of what became known as the Sarasota School of Architecture. Combining modernist construction with sleek visual lines, it stressed light, open spaces and rooms with different functions blending into one another. Its influence became international, and several buildings have reached national register designation.

Over the next two decades, numerous long-term building projects also reached fruition and laid the foundation for the way Sarasota looks today. A massive landfill undertaking routed U.S. 41, the Tamiami Trail, around the bay and created a new bayfront park. At the same time, John Ringling's original wooden causeway to Lido Key, which was badly deteriorating, gave way to a concrete version that included a draw bridge. Bonds were raised to build a modern public medical facility—Sarasota Memorial Hospital.

The infrastructure of services needed to hold pace with the expanding population. Thus, new schools were built, including Booker High School in Newtown and Riverview High School, designed by Sarasota Architecture School founder Paul Rudolph. Golf courses, libraries, churches and fire stations sprung up in and around residential developments like Gulf Gate to the south and Forest Lakes Country Club to the east.

Roads and residential development extended south through the communities of Osprey and Nokomis to Venice. In 1954, the largest planned community was started in the southernmost area of Sarasota County. Covering nearly 72 square miles it became known as North Port, Florida's third largest city in area.

The temperate climate also attracted artists, architects and writers of national prominence as year-round residents, laying the foundation for Sarasota as a cultural mecca. The Sarasota Art Association held an annual pageant that included art shows and sales.

In 1951, Cecil B. De Mille started shooting "The Greatest Show on Earth" in Sarasota, using many of the circus performers who made their home here. The film had its premiere a year later at the historical Edwards Theatre.

The early 1950s saw the formation of the West Coast Symphony of Florida. In 1952, the Ringling Museum purchased an 18th century theater from the town of Asolo in Italy. Brought over in crates and reassembled on the Ringling Museum grounds, it became the home to the Asolo Opera Association (later the Sarasota Opera), and the Asolo Theatre Company (Asolo Repertory Theatre), now Florida's largest regional theater.

Manatee Junior College in Bradenton (now Manatee Community College) opened its doors in 1957, offering tuition-free junior college education to residents of both

Sarasota bayfront at Gulf Stream Avenue, ca. 1955.

Sarasota and Manatee Counties. Seven years later saw the creation of a liberal arts college, which later became the honor college of Florida's state university system.

New College was built on land acquired from the airport and the Ringling bayfront estate. Its campus was designed by internationally famous architect I.M. Pei.

After years of planning, construction finally began in 1961 on an inland navigation route along Florida's West Coast from Tarpon Springs north of Tampa to Ft. Myers. The Intracoastal Waterway opened in 1967. Ceremonies were held at the halfway point in Venice, across from the new Ringling Brothers' circus winter headquarters, which had relocated there from Sarasota in 1959.

By 1970, the population of Sarasota and surroundings topped 100,000. But more changes were to come.

THE 1970s AND 80s

The new decade started with the opening of the Van Wezel, an 1,800-seat performing arts hall on the bay. During the next ten years, it became the hub of the city's growing number of arts and performance organizations, including the Asolo Repertory Theatre, Florida Studio Theatre and Sarasota Opera. With its modernist, lavender-hued design, the building also became an expression of Sarasota's cultural preeminence.

In 1971, a referendum approved a charter for a new county government. It gave independent authority to Sarasota County as if it were a municipality and removed it from direct influence by the State Legislature. Governance rules provided for a county commission selecting an administrator who had authority over all county departments. The county now ran its own judicial system, buses, tax assessment and collection, libraries and animal control. In the process, it also became a national leader in planning for growth by assessing impact fees, regulating the water supply and overseeing the transfer of development rights.

Two years later, a challenge in court to a system of representation that had prevented black residents of Sarasota from becoming members of the city commission prevailed, and Fred Atkins become the first black citizen to be elected to the City Board of Commissioners in 1985.

Throughout the 1970s and 80s, the area experienced phenomenal growth. By 1980, Sarasota County's population had nearly doubled to 200,000, and communities such as Venice, North Port and Longboat Key were growing as well. According to *U.S. News and World Report*, Sarasota was the fourth fastest growing metropolitan area in the nation.

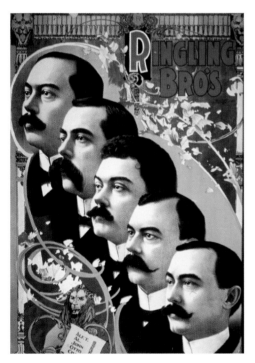 

The Ringling Brothers, (left) founders of the Ringling Bros. & Barnum and Bailey Circus, "The Greatest Show on Earth."
The annual Sarasota Art Association sidewalk sale ca. 1950.

ST. ARMANDS CIRCLE

ESTABLISHED 1926 www.starmandscircleassoc.com

Welcome to St. Armands Key—an island shopping destination nestled between the beauty of Sarasota Bay and the Gulf of Mexico. This tranquil island setting and location provide an opportunity for you to escape the pressures of everyday life and enter a world where the pace is slower and the atmosphere more relaxed. Unique in concept, history, and beauty, St. Armands provides an unforgettable experience for visitors from all over the world.

Set amidst a tropical paradise, St. Armands is an enchanting circle of upscale boutiques, distinctive shops and gourmet restaurants. Renowned as a market place with a continental flavor, it is a charming and graceful synthesis of past and present. Lush tropical plantings, courtyards and patios, antique statuary and contemporary architectural design, skillfully contribute to an international atmosphere of friendly warmth, enduring elegance and timeless style. Relax in the restaurants, and explore the shops from trinkets to treasures, gourmet snacks to candlelight feasts, you'll find it all on St. Armands Circle.

Today, more than 140 stores on St. Armands Circle pamper customers from all areas of the United States and many foreign countries, but in the early 1900's, the key was just a mangrove island too far from the small fishing village of Sarasota to attract much attention.

In 1893, Charles St. Amand, a Frenchman and first resident of the island, purchased three tracts of land totaling 131.89 acres for $21.71. He homesteaded the land, fished in the waters of the Gulf and Bay and, along with other early pioneers, raised produce, which he brought by boat to the market at City Pier in Sarasota. In later land deeds, his name was misspelled "St. Armand" and this spelling has persisted to the present day.

Visionary circus magnate John Ringling purchased the St. Armands Key property in 1917 and planned a development, which included residential lots and a shopping center laid out in a circle. As no bridge to the key had yet been built, Ringling engaged an old paddle-wheel steamboat, the "Success," to service as a work boat. His crews labored at dredging canals, building seawalls, and installing sidewalks and streets lined with rose-colored curbs. In 1925, work began on a causeway to join St. Armands Key to the mainland. Circus elephants were used to haul the huge timbers from which the bridge and causeway were built.

One year later, amid much pomp and ceremony, both the John Ringling Causeway and Ringling Estates development opened to the public, with John Ringling himself leading a parade across the causeway and his Circus Band playing from a bandstand in the center of the Circle. Every hour there was free bus service from downtown to St. Armands for prospective buyers and sightseers.

Property sales that first day were estimated to exceed one million dollars but the boom ended quickly. As the nationwide depression worsened, land sales in Florida and on St. Armands stopped completely. In 1928, the City of Sarasota accepted as a gift the causeway, which Ringling himself could no longer afford to maintain. Gradually, the wooden causeway began to rot, the Circle bandstand sagged, and the native vegetation covered the carefully planned streets and sidewalks.

For nearly 20 years, St. Armands slept. Children played ball where the bandstand once stood and only curious tourists ventured out to view the once famous key. During the 1940's, several courageous investors opened restaurants and a service station on the Circle but not until 1953 did business once again resume on St. Armands. By 1955 a number of stores had opened.

John Ringling's influence is still evident today in the planning and design of streets radiating from the circle at the island's hub and the Italian statuary from his personal collection strategically placed around the key. This shopping circle looks very much as Ringling originally envisioned it, with the palm lined medians, park-like setting, and tropical plantings he intended. Gone are the pioneer farms, vacant lots, and the bandshell featuring Sunday afternoon concerts. But the promise of greatness, the truly cosmopolitan

shopping area envisioned by John Ringling, has become a reality.

Whether you visit "the charmed Circle" for a day or stay for a lifetime, the St. Armands experience is one you won't forget. Come explore and enjoy a day of European style shopping with a gourmet lunch in a cozy café, or a romantic candlelit dinner followed by a moonlight horse and carriage ride. You won't have to travel far to find the world's treasures. They're all here on St. Armands Circle.

Also during the 80s, many new initiatives to deal with the explosive expansion of the area were realized. The expansion of the Sarasota-Bradenton Airport created a three-story terminal to attract business travelers and compete with Tampa International Airport.

In 1982, the Lindsay family that had owned the *Sarasota Herald Tribune* for three generations sold the newspaper to the New York Times Company. The change in ownership resulted in a more cosmopolitan paper that matched the growing sophistication of the city.

The mid-80s saw the completion of I-75, which relieved some of the congestion on local highways, notably the Tamiami Trail. In time, it carried more traffic and greater numbers of tourists to the region, requiring even more roads to be built.

At the same time, the impact of so many new visitors to the area, while bringing economic prosperity, also severely strained local infrastructure and the delicate ecology of the area. Unchecked development and the construction of high-profit high-rise buildings resulted in the destruction of many historic architectural treasures. People began to realize that they needed to manage growth if they wanted to retain the quality of life that made Sarasota so distinctive.

To that end, the county adopted a comprehensive plan to shape growth and development, which has been updated from time to time to respond to state mandates and public concerns.

A kind of tug-of-war began between residents who wanted to restrict development and those who wanted to keep expansion on the fast track. This struggle has continued until today and shows no sign of abating.

THE 1990s TO PRESENT

A number of environmental initiatives came at the beginning of the 1990's. The County Charter was amended to expand the existing recycling program to make it mandatory and to include cardboard, plastic and glass. Land acquisition programs, supported by a one-percent infrastructure sales tax, led to the purchase of public preserves throughout the county. In 1992, 914 acres were added to the Oscar Scherer State Park in Nokomis, giving it full park status.

During the recession of the late 1980s, downtown Sarasota became something of a ghost town. Shoppers went to St. Armands Circle and area malls.

The Downtown Association was formed to conduct seminars and redevelop the area and slowly began a turn-around. Outdoor music events started to bring people downtown at night. By the mid-90s, an abundance of new art galleries, restaurants and nightclubs revitalized the area. Renovated storefronts, landscaping and brick-paved sidewalks gave the lower Main Street area a new face.

Since then, growth downtown and throughout the county, fueled by the recent real estate boom, has been on an accelerating curve. Upscale, high-rise condos have

Looking east, towards St. Armands Circle, Plymouth Harbor, Bird Key and downtown Sarasota.

sprung up downtown and on Phillippi Creek on the South Tamiami Trail.

The Selby Public Library moved to a larger location downtown. The old drawbridge along the Ringling Causeway was replaced by a sleek fixed-span bridge. And lower Main Street was extended to U.S. 41, linking downtown to the waterfront.

Whole Foods moved into downtown as an anchor grocery store, and the area continues to flourish and grow.

The scenic Rosemary District just north of downtown Sarasota, which had fallen into disuse, became an attractive neighborhood again. With its mix of restaurants, shops and private residences in restored historic buildings and new contemporary construction, the district has become an increasingly popular destination.

The real estate boom also led to a fantastic expansion of communities throughout the county and in neighboring Manatee County. Lakewood Ranch, an old cattle ranch with extensive acreage east of I-75, has become a community unto itself, combining residential and golf course developments with business parks and shopping malls.

To the south, Venice, Nokomis, Englewood and especially North Port have grown by leaps and bounds.

Sarasota County is home to over 360,000 inhabitants. It has four major hospitals, seven colleges and universities, over 200 churches, three synagogues, eight libraries, more theaters and arts organizations than one can count, more restaurants per capita than New York's Manhattan, and 43 bank institutions.

As we move further into the 21st century, Sarasota continues to explore new directions. Downtown Sarasota was one of the first cities in the U.S. to become a Wi-Fi hot zone, making wireless Internet access universal. The Downtown Master Plan 2020, developed by famed architect and urban theorist Andres Duany, is an effort to look ahead and manage the ongoing expansion while preserving what is special and best about Sarasota's past.

Considering that Sarasota began as a small fishing community, its development and modern-day success is remarkable. Attractive, cosmopolitan and forward looking, Sarasota is very much ready for the future.

communities

communities

FEW COUNTIES IN FLORIDA CAN BOAST AS MANY stellar qualities as Sarasota. Combining great physical beauty, world-renowned beaches, a vibrant art and cultural scene, one of the best education systems in Florida, and a host of opportunities for recreation and leisure activities, the area has attracted tourists and year-round residents for more than a hundred years. The temperate climate and sunshine also help.

No wonder that in recognition of its many amenities and lifestyle, Sarasota County received the prestigious All-American City Award from the National Civic League in 2006.

With four municipalities—the cities of Sarasota, Venice and North Port, and the town of Longboat Key—as well as numerous unincorporated areas within its boundaries, Sarasota County offers visitors and full-time residents a variety of communities to call home.

From quilt making skills of yesteryear (top) to present day high-rise resort living.

From high-rise condos and hotels downtown to motels and beach front bungalows, from single family dwellings inland to apartment buildings and suburban-style neighborhoods, there are rentals and places to own for every taste and wallet. Sarasota is a place where you can live, work and play in the same general vicinity because it's easy to get around. The 18.4-minute commute time to and from work is one of the shortest of any metropolitan area in the nation.

The 358,000 people who live in the county make up a large mosaic of ethnic diversity. Starting with the Scottish origins of the early Sarasota settlers, the area is home to people of Irish, German, Polish, Italian and French ancestry. Jewish, African-American, Hispanic and other nationalities can be found throughout the county. Their presence is also reflected by the many fraternal organizations such as the German American Social Club of Sarasota, the Caledonian Society and St. Andrews Society of Sarasota, the Sons of Italy and the Italian American Club of Venice, to name a few.

The variety and number of churches and other religious dwellings indicate a diverse religious affiliation among the county's inhabitants. Evangelical and mainline Protestants, including Baptists, Methodists and Presbyterians, make up the largest percentage of denominations, with Catholics numbering a close second. A substantial Jewish population worships in synagogues throughout Sarasota and Venice. Some congregations are concentrated in a particular area. A group of Amish and Mennonite residents lives in Sarasota along Bahia Vista Street east of Tuttle Street. Furthermore, Muslims, Bahá'i, Buddhists, Greek Orthodox, Episcopalians, Unitarians and New Thought spiritual communities all have their places of worship.

Sophistication and small town Florida charm characterizes all the cities, towns and unincorporated communities in the county and surrounding region. At the same time, each municipality has its own unique personality, providing variety and diversity throughout the region.

THE CITY OF SARASOTA

The City of Sarasota combines easy-going charm of a small community with the energetic sophistication of a large metropolitan area. Few cities in America can lay claim to such a vibrant cultural scene, luxury high-rises

HOMES BY TOWNE®

ESTABLISHED 1949 www.homesbytowne.com

Quality, Exceptional Design and Value

Set amongst the peaceful lakes, lush woodlands and natural preserves of Sarasota/Manatee county are the beautiful single-family homes and condominiums from Homes by Towne®. The majestic natural amenities of the area are the perfect backdrop for these distinctive homes.

For over fifty years, Homes by Towne® has measured success by providing homeowners with quality, exceptional design and value in every home they build. As proof of their commitment, they have been awarded multiple Aurora Awards as well as Best in Customer Service three years in a row for outstanding customer service. The award-winning sales and construction teams remain committed to their customers by offering exceptional, value priced homes that are located in the most sought-after communities.

Homes by Towne® began building in Bradenton, Florida in 1994 as one of the founding builders in Lakewood Ranch. Since that time, they have built homes in 13 single-family neighborhoods and 6 multi-family neighborhoods in Lakewood Ranch and the surrounding area.

The company is currently developing single-family homes in GreyHawk Landing as well as two neighborhoods in The Village of Greenbrook, Greenbrook Ravines and Greenbrook Preserve. GreyHawk Landing's exclusive amenities include a huge lagoon-style pool with water slides, a fitness center, basketball and tennis courts, fishing dock, soccer and softball fields and wilderness trails. This beautiful, gated community provides an exciting lifestyle in a natural environment.

Both of the communities in The Village of Greenbrook offer beautiful lake and preserve views that highlight their spacious, award-winning home designs. Along with the 20-acre Adventure Park, the convenience of shopping, recreational activities and quality schools make the Village of Greenbrook a perfect place to live!

The newest luxury waterfront condominium, WaterCrest, is located in Edgewater Village at Lakewood Ranch along picturesque Lake Uihlein. This private, gated community offers a beautifully appointed two-story clubhouse complete with a state-of-the-art fitness room and a heated lap pool and spa. WaterCrest's unmatched location within Lakewood Ranch is central to all of life's conveniences, including upscale shopping on Main Street.

Homes by Towne's® past, present and future has been, and will continue to be, built on their commitment to quality, exceptional design, value and service. They look forward to the opportunity of building new homes that exceed expectations.

FIRST BAPTIST CHURCH OF SARASOTA

ESTABLISHED 1902 **www.firstsarasota.org**

As wise men of old have said, a great journey begins with a single step. The earliest beginnings of First Baptist Church of Sarasota literally began with such a single step. On March 23, 1902, Isaac Redd, sixty-seven years old at the time, took a two-hour walk from the Bee Ridge area of Southwest Florida to the tiny hamlet called Sarasota to meet with five individuals that helped lay the foundation for a brand new Baptist church. That church would become known as the First Baptist Church of Sarasota and those early visionaries were the Rev. Henry Messer, his wife Keziah, James Bates, and Hayman and Patsy Dancy. The very first pastor was Rev. P.O. Miller.

Not having a building of their own, the local Methodist church kindly offered the use of their church building for this fledgling Baptist congregation, meeting on Sunday afternoons. Three years later, the first building of the new congregation was completed on the south side of present day Second Street near Central Avenue. Historical records show it as Eighth Street, but all numbered streets were renamed in the 1940's and we know it today as Second Street. Major encouragement came from member William Worth who joined the church in 1903 and owned Worth Grocery.

The first church was a one-room white frame building. It had a bell tower, with a genuine bell that called the members of the church to worship since they all lived within easy walking distance. Soon the Sunday School enrollment was numbering forty. After the organization of the Sunday School, the next organization was the Ladies' Aid Society.

This group raised the money to purchase the very first pulpit Bible. In 1914, a pastorium was added next door to the church. It welcomed the ninth pastor of the church, Rev. J.R. Henry. The living room also served as a Sunday School classroom for the Junior Girls Bible study class.

By 1919 the one-room building had become too small for the growing congregation. With the arrival of new pastor, Dr. A.J. Beck, the congregation decided in 1920

to purchase a building site at Main Street and Adelia for the grand total of $2,500, just in time, as the population of Sarasota grew from 3,000 to 25,000 during the next six years! Today, called the Chapel and employing Neoclassical Revival Style, First Baptist built a new sanctuary on the property purchased at Main Street & Adelia. The church dedicated the new sanctuary, along with a $30,000 pipe organ and beautiful stained glass windows on December 14, 1924. The old church building was donated to the Bethlehem Baptist Church on Central Avenue, Sarasota's first African-American Baptist Church.

Under the able tutelage of Dr. W.R. Hamilton, the leadership of First Baptist Church saw the need for the addition of its present sanctuary. A Sanctuary building committee was commissioned in 1958 with a formal building committee named in 1959. They recommended that architects Kannenberg and Hanebuth draw up plans for the new sanctuary. Contractor William A. Berbusse, Jr. won the construction bid of $635,000. On May 29, 1962, the cornerstone of the new Georgian Colonial Style sanctuary was laid with the first worship service being held on the Sunday before Christmas, 1962 and the formal dedication was held on February 3, 1963, with the addition of a Family Life Center and a Children's Educational wing occurring in 1980. First Baptist Church purchased its first property on the southside of Main Street in 2001 when it bought the two-story office building at Main Street. This facility was totally remodeled in 2004 and serves as the ministries offices and main hall for receptions and additional Bible study rooms.

First Baptist has been instrumental in the starting of many of the Baptist Churches that minister to the greater Sarasota area. Bay Haven Baptist (originally Second Baptist Church), Southside Baptist Church, Mt. Calvary Baptist Church, Kensington Park Baptist Church, Gulf Gate Baptist Church (today Gulf Gate Church), as well as several language congregations, have been birthed by the First Baptist Church of Sarasota.

Under the leadership of present Pastor William H. Hild, Jr., First Baptist purchased an additional piece of property in January 2006, located immediately east of the church on Main Street. This purchase was the largest in the history of First Baptist Church, further cementing its 105-year history of ministry, evangelism, and worship to the greater Sarasota community. It finds its ministry blessed by God in amazing ways with an ever growing sense of enthusiasm to proclaim the "...riches of Christ," to the hundreds of thousands who call Sarasota home.

and single family residences, a spate of elegant shops and restaurants, a scenic harbor, and stunning white sand beaches, all within a three-mile radius.

The sheer beauty of the bayfront with its graceful bridge heading out to the keys is often captured in photographs by tourists and on magazine covers. Additionally, the rich tropical flora gives the city a great deal of natural beauty. There are 49 parks sprinkled throughout the city and its keys. Numerous varieties of palm trees, live oaks and pines shade the neighborhoods. Yellow trumpet trees, purple jacarandas, red-hued crepe myrtle trees, and pink and white oleander bushes line streets and avenues and show off their flowers in stunning bursts of color at various times during the year.

The downtown theater district features two equity theaters, an opera house and the Van Wezel Performing Arts Center, which brings performing artists from all over the world. The Hollywood 20, a large movie cineplex and the art house Burns Court Cinema enhance Sarasota's cultural scene. Upscale restaurants and music venues like the Gator Club on Main Street ensure a bustling night life.

A recent real estate and building boom has resulted in new luxury high-rise condos sprouting up downtown next to the historic buildings dating back to the 1920s and before. Old Mediterranean-style architecture can be seen next to Florida School of Architecture buildings and modern edifices, such as the new Herald Tribune Media Group headquarters on Main Street. The result is an eclectic collage of Florida building history and 21st-century visionary design.

A variety of neighborhoods offer unusual characteristics. Towles Court is a thriving, colorful arts colony of restored 1920s bungalows. Historic Burns Court and the Rosemary District mix two and three-story residential buildings with ground floor restaurants, galleries and stores. Farther out, neighborhoods such as Laurel Park, Glen Oaks Estates, Gillespie Park and Alta Vista combine single family homes and apartments in suburban-like settings. Bird Key, a private gated island community on Sarasota Bay, has been a sought after address for some time with million-dollar homes and residents like television host Jerry Springer, tennis champion Mary Pierce, and AC/DC's lead singer Brian Johnson.

In 1997, the City Commission created the Neighborhood Development Department to give residents a voice in making quality-of-life improvements. As a result, the city has 54 active neighborhood organizations, which act as networking groups, hold festivals and block parties, and express their concerns at meetings of the city commission.

Downtown high-rise apartments (left) overlooking the marina; and a Jacaranda tree in bloom.

FIDELITY HOMES

ESTABLISHED 2000 www.fidelityhomes.net

FAITH
INTEGRITY
DEDICATION
ETHICS
LOYALTY
INTENSITY
TRUTH
YOU

Innovators

Since its launch in the summer of 2000, Fidelity Homes has enjoyed resounding success, with satisfied customers, an impressive sales record, and recognition from local and national sources both in and outside of the homebuilding industry. Fidelity's success stems from its reputation for thinking creatively, being innovators and completing projects with a level of quality and consistency that is unmatched in the industry.

Changing the face of Sarasota

With this winning formula, Fidelity discovered opportunities in downtown revitalization efforts in nearby Sarasota. In 2001, Fidelity Homes launched its Renaissance Collection to help restore the historical charm of the district. Reminiscent of Addison Mizner's Mediterranean concept, and featuring bungalow craftsman designs, the homes were fashioned in a vintage style with tile roofs, front porches and stone columns, and upgraded with granite, marble, custom moldings and historic detailing. These luxurious custom homes

were built in Sarasota's historic "West of the Trail" district, an area featuring some of the city's oldest homes and most desirable neighborhoods.

University Groves

University Groves is the latest endeavor for Fidelity Homes. The new 142-acre residential and retail master-planned community is located near Sarasota, in one of the areas fastest-growing neighborhoods, and will include components such as a medical center, restaurants and retail shops. Fidelity will build 68 single-family homes and 78 town homes, with internationally

known contractor W.G. Mills. The single-family homes will range in size from 1,900 to more than 3,000 square feet of living area; town homes range from 1,600 to 2,300 square feet of living area.

Business Philosophy

Complete satisfaction drives everything they do, and how they do it. They listen to the needs of each and every customer, satisfy those needs fully, and strive to create a working partnership with their customers to do whatever is best in their individual situation.

If this doesn't sound typical of a builder, you're right... it isn't. It's Fidelity Homes.

Casual dining and entertainment on Lido Beach.

SIESTA, LIDO, ST. ARMANDS AND LONGBOAT KEYS

Across the bay from the City of Sarasota are a number of barrier islands. Originally the vacation land for Florida's indigenous Indians—shell mounds have been found suggesting that picnicking and fish fries were favorite activities—they have become a tropical playground for tourists and year-round residents. The three largest, Siesta Key, Lido and Longboat Key, facing the Gulf of Mexico, are known throughout the world for their beautiful white sand beaches.

Siesta Key, the southernmost of the barrier islands, was the earliest settled. In 1906, Captain Louis Roberts and his wife Ocean Hansen Roberts enlarged their house and began calling it the Roberts Hotel. Ocean Boulevard, Roberts Road and Hansen Bayou are named after them. In 1917, the first Siesta Key bridge was built, connecting the mainland with the northern shore of the key. Nine years later, a second bridge followed on Stickney Point Road. Since then, the key has been gradually settled without the disruption and

destruction to the environment that often accompanies sudden development. As a result, beautiful old trees overhang the avenues, canals, boulevards and houses. Scenic Siesta Key Village with its shops, restaurants and bungalow motels harks back to the times when the island was a fisherman's cove. One of the famous residents was John D. MacDonald, author of *Condominium* and the Travis McGee detective novels, who wrote more than 70 books while living on the island during the 1960s. Like many other visitors, he cherished the beauty of the island, including Crescent Beach, which attracts visitors from all over the world each year. At the "Great International White Sand Beach Challenge" held in 1987, it was recognized for having the "whitest and finest sand in the world."

Across from Siesta Key's northern tongue lies Lido Key. With beautiful beaches facing the Gulf of Mexico and a park on its southern tip, Lido Key is a tropical paradise of great natural beauty. At the same time, St. Armands Key, which is nestled up against it on the bayside, has a large European-style traffic circle with elegant shops, specialty stores and restaurants within walking distance of beachfront hotels. In the 1880s, when Scottish settlers arrived in Sarasota, Lido Key was just a small island where fishermen made camp, but there were no permanent residents. It wasn't until the 1920s, when John Ringling purchased Lido, St. Armands and Bird Key, that development began. Ringling built a wooden causeway that connected the keys to Sarasota and named the streets on Lido Key after American presidents. He also built a large swimming pool, which is still there, and there are plans in the works to repair and re-open it. In time, Ringling's vision for St. Armands to be an international shopping destination came to fruition, while Lido Key has become a major draw for vacationers from all over the world.

Longboat Key, a ten-mile narrow sliver, spans both Sarasota and Manatee Counties. The northern end was settled first, and some of the homes built in the early 1900s are still standing. The southern end, however, is dotted with upscale condominium high-rises. Gulf of Mexico Drive, which traverses the island from one end to another is beautifully landscaped with pink oleanders and lively, colorful impatiens. The Town of Longboat Key was incorporated in 1955. Development began gradually, but accelerated in the 1960s and 1970s. For a while, Longboat Key Towers, two twelve-story condominium buildings, stood alone on the Gulf side beach. Now virtually every acre of land has been developed, leaving very few privately-owned tracts of land. With world-class beach resorts, two golf courses, and many high-end condo residences, Longboat Key is the luxury barrier island of Sarasota.

VENICE

Located on the lower Gulf Coast, 20 miles south of Sarasota, Venice is the second oldest city in the county. Known as the "Shark's Tooth Capital of the World" because of the many fossilized shark's teeth that can be found on its beaches, it is both a tourist mecca and retirement community appreciated for its relaxed atmosphere and physical beauty. With its picturesque harbor, bays and other waterways, and generous access to the Gulf—it is the only city in the county without a barrier island—Venice is a veritable water wonderland, offering opportunities for swimming, surfing, fishing and boating.

Although settled in the 1880s, Venice came of age in the mid-1920s during the first great Florida land boom. Dr. Fred Albee, an orthopedic surgeon, hired city planner John Nolan to layout a city on his extensive land holdings. As a result, Venice is one of the earliest planned U.S. cities with wide avenues and Northern Italian style buildings. For a time, the city was the winter headquarters for the Ringling Brothers Barnum and Bailey Circus. Walter Farley, the author of the beloved "Black Stallion" books made Venice his home.

Construction of the Intracoastal Waterway in 1963 made an island of the picturesque downtown commercial district. The rest of the city extends to the east and south, and new developments and communities are springing up past I-75. Today, Venice takes pride in its splendid beaches, preserved natural environments, arts fests and parades. The city is served by a daily newspaper, *The Venice Gondolier*, and boasts a nationally award-winning community theater.

NORTH PORT

Occupying the southeastern quadrant of Sarasota County, the City of North Port is the third largest in area in Florida. Incorporated in 1959, it is mostly a suburban city of single family residences. Recent years have

The beautiful waters of the Gulf of Mexico surround the greater Sarasota area.

brought explosive growth. From 2000 to 2006, North Port more than doubled its population, making it the fastest growing city in the state. The latest estimates put its population mark past 50,000, ensuring that it will be the largest city in the county surpassing Sarasota by the next census. Much of its attraction is due to desirable and affordable housing. There are also amenities, such as golf courses, schools, a county library branch, a Performing Arts Center, and the Warm Mineral Springs, whose constant 87-degree temperature attracts visitors from around the world. At the same time, North Port supports business and industry with the development of new commerce and office parks, which earned it Blue Chip Status by the Florida Department of Commerce.

LAKEWOOD RANCH

An award-winning master-planned community, Lakewood Ranch is located east of I-75 on the Sarasota-Manatee county line. Started in 1994, the 7,000-acre development comprises five residential villages with

Michael has been joined by her son, Drayton, in leading the real estate company that bears her name.

MICHAEL SAUNDERS & COMPANY

ESTABLISHED 1976 www.michaelsaunders.com

Transforming The Real Estate Industry With Unparalleled Excellence And Cutting-Edge Customer Service.

Things have definitely changed in Southwest Florida since Michael Saunders first hung her shingle on a small real estate office on St. Armands Circle in Sarasota more than thirty years ago. Other things most definitely have not. And will not.

Back then, very little in the way of first-class full service existed, or was even expected, in a real estate office. Although it was challenging at best for a woman to open a business in those days, an undeterred Michael Saunders saw things differently. With a small loan of $5,000, co-signed by a customer, because a woman acting on her own behalf could not qualify for a loan back then, she proceeded to open Michael Saunders & Company, an event destined to transform the luxury real estate industry. The results are a modern real estate enterprise that is regarded internationally as a paragon of prestige marketing, cutting-edge technology and unparalleled professionalism—not to mention the type of first-class full service that every client and customer deserves.

Over the years, Michael Saunders & Company has blossomed from that single small office into a regional network of 18 full-service offices strategically placed throughout all four corners of the market with global partnerships that extend the company's marketing influence well beyond Florida's borders to a worldwide audience of qualified buyers. From Anna Maria Island to Boca Grande and from the Gulf of Mexico to the ranches and groves of eastern Manatee County, Michael Saunders & Company lists more properties and brings more buyers to the closing table than its next three closest competitors combined. This has enormous benefits for buyers who can walk into any of their offices and preview the most comprehensive selection of listings for neighborhoods throughout the area. A home listed through their Venice office may appeal to an overseas buyer who walks into their Longboat Key office, and vice versa. With such an extensive network of high-profile locations to serve hundreds of thousands of full- and part-time residents, not to mention thousands of annual visitors from around the world, the opportunities to sell your home are limitless.

One of the most noteworthy developments in modern real estate marketing is the swift emergence of the Internet as the principle portal through which more than 80 percent of today's homebuyers now begin their search for properties. Ten years ago, that number was a scant two percent.

Because Michael Saunders recognized this trend from its earliest beginnings, they've spared no expense over the intervening years to make www.michaelsaunders.com the most useful, user-friendly and content-rich Web experience in this or any other industry. The area's most clicked-on website for residential real estate, your home will enjoy a level of Internet exposure far beyond the reach of any other competing agency.

As proud as they are of their Web superiority, the personal touch still rules the day at Michael Saunders & Company. For as important as the Internet is, it is also a fact, according to the National Association of Realtors, that 72% of Internet buyers and 63% of traditional buyers were first exposed to

the home they ultimately purchased by their real estate agent. That's why they hire and train the most talented professionals in the industry to work on your behalf.

Michael Saunders & Company is proud to be home to more than 500 of the market's most accomplished sales professionals. Each associate's average of $5.99 million in annual sales has propelled the company to 9th in the nation for individual agent productivity.

Thanks to a lifetime spent in the community and the last thirty-plus years running her company, Michael Saunders has sat squarely at the epicenter of one of Florida's fastest growing and most affluent regions. Change in the Sunshine State comes at a dizzying pace, but none more dizzying than the growth that has shaped Southwest Florida over the past ten years. One of the surest barometers of that growth is the parallel expansion of Michael Saunders & Company during the same period.

In 1995, the company had an annual sales volume of just over $274 million. Ten years later that volume had exploded eleven-fold, rocketing upward to the tune of $3.07 billion.

As much as Sarasota continues to evolve, certain traditions are not subject to change. For one thing, while other real estate companies have learned to trim services and cut corners under the guise of operating with greater efficiency, Michael Saunders & Company will never sacrifice service to shore up the bottom line. The mission upon which the company was founded back in 1976 remains sharply defined and unshakeable: to be a full service real estate organization dedicated to a longstanding tradition of excellence, professionalism and integrity with a focus on delivering an exceptional real estate experience to all clients and customers. If that means they have to work harder and stay smarter to dominate the cutting edge of customer service, then so be it.

Visitors to michaelsaunders.com are treated to the most user-friendly, content real estate Web address in the area.

Since opening her doors in 1976, Michael Saunders has built her company to become the leading real estate brokerage on Florida's Gulf Coast

BAY VILLAGE OF SARASOTA

ESTABLISHED 1972 **www.bayvillage.org**

With a well-earned reputation as the area's finest retirement community, Bay Village provides a tower of luxury living choices for retired couples and singles. Included are spacious studio apartments as well as one and two-bedroom apartment residences.

Bay Village is set amid 15 lush acres of beautiful park-like surroundings with a lovely lake, walking paths and abundant native wildlife. Great blue herons, great white and snowy egrets, night herons and wild ducks are regular visitors while mockingbirds and cardinals serenade early morning risers.

In addition to being introduced into a carefree luxury lifestyle, new residents are greeted and welcomed as valued members of our Bay Village family. Warm relations and many enduring friendships are formed.

Residents enjoy casual as well as fine dining in Bay Village's newly redecorated dining room. Diners select from a menu of delicious choices for breakfast, lunch and dinner served by a friendly professional staff.

Beautifully decorated lounges are perfect for social gatherings. A regular calendar of educational and entertainment programs provides a full schedule of social and enrichment activities. A comfortable auditorium equipped with a state-of-the-art sound system is the setting for a rich variety of entertainment and cultural programs.

In addition to the beautiful outdoor heated swimming pool and our own putting green, Bay Village features a fully equipped fitness center, an extensive library, private bowling alley, gift shop and beauty salon, Bay Village's own bank branch and a convenient country store are also available.

The blue waters and white sand beaches of the Gulf of Mexico are only minutes away

from your door. You may also leave the driving to the Bay Village staff. Private Bay Village transportation provides regular trips to downtown and Sarasota's many attractions. There you can enjoy theater, concerts, opera, stage shows, museum visits and a fascinating variety of other entertainment and cultural opportunities. Residents are also invited to participate in specially arranged luxury cruise groups, educational trips and other planned activities.

In addition to independent living accommodations, assisted living, skilled nursing and home health care are available at Bay Village. The Bay Village Health Center is one of only 14 nursing homes in the entire State of Florida to be honored with the Governor's Gold Seal Award of Approval for the period from November 24, 2006 through November 23, 2008. This honor had previously been awarded to Bay Village from November 24, 2004 through November 23, 2006.

Since 1987, Bay Village has held the coveted accreditation by the Continuing Care Accreditation Commission. Year after year, Bay Village has also been named "Best Retirement Community" by area media.

Bay Village was founded in Sarasota in 1972 by members of the Pine Shores Presbyterian Church, and it welcomes residents of all races and religions. Since its establishment, Bay Village has been dedicated to a continuing modernization program so that it maintains its reputation as the area's finest and most up-to-date retirement community.

Bay Village...Where the good life gets better.

Those interested in more information may call to arrange for a personal tour or visit the Bay Village of Sarasota website.

LAKEWOOD RANCH

ESTABLISHED 1996 www.lakewoodranch.com

All the comforts of home, with the past and future at your doorstep...

Lakewood Ranch is the master-planned community that is part of the vibrant Schroeder-Manatee Ranch (SMR), a 100-year-old working ranch and agricultural enterprise. Thousands now call Lakewood Ranch their new home town. This growing and thriving community offers a coveted quality of life that includes world-class golf, quiet neighborhood streets and a connection to Florida's natural beauty.

Located just east of Interstate 75, residents in this community live in a world apart, with no need to travel far to find the best of everything — homes, employment, restaurants, schools, shopping, doctors' offices and more. This close-knit community comes with the benefits of a well-planned development. Schools, grocery stores and roads are built prior to demand. Land is donated or sold at discounted rates for some schools, children's centers, non-profit agencies and public safety. These things make daily life more pleasant and are just a few of the benefits that come with calling this place home.

The developers of Lakewood Ranch respect the SMR heritage and continue the tradition of making development fit the land, not the land fit development. For example, in 2002, the company worked with Sarasota County to preserve nearly 2,000 acres of environmentally sensitive land and assumed responsibility for maintaining and managing the protected property in perpetuity as an environmental asset.

Vast acreage has been set aside for wildlife sanctuaries and connected, safe corridors for animals because many creatures also call the Ranch home. Residents enjoy safe walks and bike rides along the more than 100 miles of interconnected trails, sidewalks and paths at Lakewood Ranch. There are extensive nature preserves, a restored 451-acre wetland preserve, hundreds of acres of man-made lakes and even a gopher tortoise preserve!

To further the commitment to environmental stewardship, Lakewood Ranch has gone through the extensive process of earning the Florida Green Building Coalition's "Green" designation. Lakewood Ranch is proudly leading the way as the largest "Green" community in the country. All homes built since 2004 meet these Green Building standards.

Lakewood Ranch is a community for today that grows from deep roots nourished by uncompromising commitment to the decades ahead. Here, your cowboy boots fit perfectly between your wingtips and golf shoes. That's the nature of Lakewood Ranch and certainly, the Nature of Florida Living.

LAKEWOOD RANCH
COMMERCIAL REALTY

ESTABLISHED 1996 www.lwrcommercial.com

Lakewood Ranch Commercial Realty is a full-service commercial real estate brokerage organization that specializes in the award-winning community of Lakewood Ranch, located in the desirable Sarasota/Bradenton region of Southwest Florida. Lakewood Ranch Commercial Realty is an industry leader with a strong reputation in Florida commercial real estate; including the sale and lease of office space, industrial parks, hotels, medical office, retail space and more.

Lakewood Ranch is a 33,000-acre master-planned community, which includes all aspects of residential and mixed-use commercial development. This one-of-a-kind environment combines close-knit residential villages with a multitude of amenities including convenient shopping, great schools (public and private), daycare centers, hotels, top-notch medical facilities, jobs and commercial opportunities.

Lakewood Ranch is home to over 600 local and national businesses, including many corporate headquarters such as GE Infrastructure Security, FCCI Insurance Group, Gemesis, Gevity HR, John Cannon Homes, Lee Wetherington Homes, Miles Media Group, Neal Communities, Pruett Builders, Roper Industries and Schroeder-Manatee Ranch, Inc. (SMR) to name a few.

All business park locations within Lakewood Ranch are designed on historic Florida ranch land carefully enriched by wetlands, preserves and lakes. Business centers known as Town Center, Corporate Park, Business Park and Commerce Park total over 4,000,000 SF of commercial space, including 2,500,000 SF of office space, 850,000 SF retail space, 600,000 SF light industrial, and 300,000 SF of medical space.

Each year these numbers grow, as a combined 300,000 SF of commercial product is added within the Ranch.

Main Street at Lakewood Ranch, a lifestyle shopping center, includes 120,000 SF of specialty retail stores, restaurants, residential condominiums and 46,000 SF of Class-A office space. Main Street also includes Lakewood Ranch Cinemas, a 6-screen movie theater developed by the Sarasota Film Society.

Future expansion plans include the development of a 300 acre mixed-use center located just north of SR 70, which will provide the community with multiple entertainment venues, as well as residential, retail and commercial opportunities.

Sales and leasing opportunities within all business parks and mixed-use centers are currently available. Opportunities include Class-A office locations, along with several options for retail, flex/warehouse space and medical offices. All which are conveniently located within minutes from major roadways and area amenities. Land sales and build-to-suit opportunities are also available. Lakewood Ranch is located on the county line of Sarasota and Manatee on Florida's West Coast. Its proximity to I-75 makes it the perfect high-productivity location to reach other Florida destinations, with easy access to two international airports and two seaports; and approximately an hour south of the Tampa/St. Petersburg area.

nature preserves, parks and lakes, and designated areas for education, business, retail and medical services. Homes range from $400,000 to more than $1 million. There are 150 miles of sidewalks and trails for walking, jogging, riding and rollerblading. Recreational facilities include 54 holes of championship golf courses, 36 of which are private at private clubs, as well as well-healed tennis courts, swimming pools and fitness spas. Three commercial parks feature retail, office and professional spaces with state-of-the art telephone and technology. Artfully designed and landscaped retail, restaurant and shopping areas like Town Center and Main Street attract visitors from other parts of the county. It all adds up to a comfortable, 21st century living experience with all amenities included.

UNINCORPORATED AREAS

Although the City of Sarasota occupies a relatively small area of the total county, it is surrounded by unincorporated areas, some of them census-designated places. From the northeast corner of the county, along the east-west arteries of Bahia Vista Street and Fruitville Road, Bee Ridge and Clark Roads, and to the south where Macintosh Boulevard and U.S. 41 intersect, all residents consider themselves Sarasotans.

Further to the south, however, are three unincorporated areas with their own names and history. Osprey, Nokomis and Englewood all were settled in the mid to late 1800s. Ethnically diverse, their population includes English, Irish and Italian descendants, with residents of German ancestry making up more than 20 percent in all three communities.

Osprey begins just to the south of Macintosh Boulevard and U.S. 41. Scenically located along Little Sarasota Bay with Casey Key as a barrier island, it is named after the large maritime hawk that feeds on fish. The area was settled in 1867 by the Webb family from New York, who named their new home "Spanish Point." Later, Bertha Palmer, the Chicago business woman who at some point owned nearly a third of Sarasota County, had her winter estate, "Osprey Point," there and planned to build a home called "The Oaks." Today, the name lives on as "The Oaks Club," a 1,000-acre, upscale

Lakewood Ranch boasts championship golf courses.

golf course community on the east and west sides of U.S. 41, which is considered one of the county's premiere living communities. Osprey also is home to Pine View School, Sarasota County's public school for gifted students grade 2 through 12. In 2006, *Newsweek* magazine listed Pine View as one of the 21 Public Elite American high schools. Other attractions include Oscar Scherer State Park and Historic Spanish Point, where visitors can explore Florida's prehistoric past, pioneer days and the estate of Bertha Palmer.

Nokomis, a small historic town just to the north of Venice, is best known for its beach, Sarasota County's oldest public beach. Located on Casey Key just west of the Albee Road Bridge, it covers 22 acres, which run along both sides of the barrier island, providing public access to both the Gulf of Mexico and the Intracoastal Waterway. Casey Key, where beachfront houses are worth millions of dollars, has a concentration of the wealthiest homes in the county and has such famous winter-time residents as the author Stephen King.

Straddling two counties, Englewood extends from the south end of Sarasota County on Lemon Bay into the western portion of Charlotte County. Originally a small fishing village, the community was first settled in 1878; and while it has grown to more than 16,000 year-round residents, it still retains a quiet, unspoiled sense of old Florida. Manasota Key, the narrow barrier island that runs along the Gulf Coast, has four beaches and parks for fishing, bird watching and maritime activities. There are golf courses, tennis clubs and two large sports and recreation complexes. The local Chamber of Commerce is quite active, representing more than 700 businesses. Old Englewood Village on Dearborn Street downtown has galleries, shops and restaurants housed in historic buildings that convey the homey flavor of what life there was like over 100 years ago.

Events such as the Fourth of July fireworks bring a sense of community to the Greater Sarasota area.

BRADENTON

With a population of 53,000, Bradenton, Manatee County's largest city, lies directly north of Sarasota. It was named after Dr. Joseph Braden, one of the early settlers who grew sugar cane on his extensive land holdings. Nestled along the southern shore of the Manatee River, Bradenton has many cultural and historical attractions and recreational opportunities, including 25 world-class golf courses. Nearby Anna Maria Island on the Gulf Coast has popular beaches and quaint restaurants, motels and marinas. The downtown area by the Manatee River, including the historic cobblestone Main Street, is undergoing massive development, with numerous high-rise residential and office building projects in the works. A few blocks inland, the Village of the Arts, whose renovated residential houses contain shops, art galleries and studios, is well worth a visit. For another unique shopping experience, there is the Red Barn Flea Market & Plaza, which features more than 600 retail stores and flea-market style booths.

Because of the Nick Bollettieri Tennis Academy, many international tennis stars have called Bradenton home. Andre Agassi, Jim Courier and Monica Seles all went to high school there, as did soccer player Freddy Adu. Current celebrities living there include Maria Sharapova, golfer Paul Azinger and sportscaster Dick Vitale.

Anchored by Tropicana Products, best known for producing orange juice, Bradenton has developed an attractive business climate as well. National companies, including Champs Sports and Bealls Department Stores, have their headquarters there. A highly respected school system and post-secondary educational institutions such as Manatee Community College, make the city attractive to both jobseekers and businesses locating to the area.

education

education

SARASOTA HAS PLACED A HIGH PREMIUM ON education from its beginnings as a community. As early as 1878, Caroline Abbe, the daughter of the first postmaster, started a school in an abandoned fishing shack. The first frame school in town was built in 1904 and opened with 124 pupils and four teachers. A brick high school, the pride of the community, soon followed.

Education took other forms as well. The Women's Club, for example, known

primarily for its civil service, also promoted informal learning among its members.

In 1927, to accommodate the growing student population during the first Florida real estate boom, Sarasota High School on the South Tamiami Trail was erected. Because there was no bridge to Tampa then, the school's sports teams had to travel by boat to compete with Tampa, earning them the name "The Sailors." Today, students attend new expanded facilities on School Avenue behind the original building, which is undergoing renovation to become a satellite branch of the Ringling College of Art and Design with studios, office space and a contemporary art museum.

As the region grows into a 21st century cosmopolitan area, Sarasota and environs continue to support a variety of education systems for primary, secondary, collegiate, continuing and adult learning.

PUBLIC AND PRIVATE SCHOOLS

The Sarasota County School System now has 58 primary and secondary schools with an enrollment of 41,405 students attended to by 2,769 full-time teachers. With an annual budget of over 400 million dollars, it is the county's largest employer. Offering a wide variety of programs for both gifted and talented and special needs students, the schools strive for high achievement and success. More than half of the teachers have master's degrees, outdistancing the state average by a considerable margin.

Numerous initiatives, most recently a Campaign for Excellence, promote high student achievement in reading, writing, math, science technology and career preparation, as well as encouraging citizenship, family and community involvement. An ambitious five-year plan, NeXt Generation Learning, is exploring a number of options, including school within schools learning environments, to better prepare students for college and future careers.

To take advantage of technological advances, the education system has 13,000 computers throughout the schools, representing a ratio of one computer to every three students. Sarasota had the first high school in the nation to use cutting-edge computer technology to ensure mastery of science subjects.

There are gifted resource programs in all schools. Pine View School, which offers a full-time gifted and talented program for students grade 2-12, has achieved a national reputation for excellence. There are also 38 magnet schools and magnet programs, as well as 15 alternative and charter schools, such as the Sarasota Military Academy, Sarasota School of Arts and Sciences, Sarasota Suncoast Academy, and the Sarasota Technical Institute.

Each high school focuses on a special honors curriculum, such as MAST (Math and Science Technology) at Sarasota High, IB (International Baccalaureate) at Riverview, and VPA (Visual and Performing Arts) at Booker. Riverview's music program is one of only four high schools listed in the Music Demonstration School project of the Florida Music Educators' Association, and its Kiltie Band with uniforms reflecting the area's Scottish heritage has performed throughout the United States, including the Macy's Thanksgiving Day Parade in New York City.

The Sarasota County Technical Institute (SCTI) provides career and technical education to both high school students and adults. The 30-year old institution offers both regular and online classes in a wide variety of areas, from agribusiness to automotive, legal and health programs, as well as a number of service related courses.

The Sarasota County School District also engages in county-wide partnerships with many institutions in the arts community, including the Van Wezel Performing Arts Hall, Florida Studio Theatre and Florida West Coast Symphony. An environmental science program with Mote Marine Laboratory & Aquarium offers instruction and off-shore exploration in marine biology. Other cooperative programs are connected with Marie

Scholars and students sharing information and technology.

JULIE ROHR ACADEMY

ESTABLISHED 1974 www.julierohracademy.com

Julie Rohr Academy opened in 1974 as a small day care center with seventeen pre-school children. Since that time it has developed into a fully accredited private school for nursery through middle school students with an emphasis on the performing arts. The faculty strives to provide the students with strong academic skills, problem-solving techniques, performing arts experiences, athletic activities and emotional security. It is the Academy's goal to prepare the students to become capable, cooperative, contributing members of society.

The philosophy of Julie Rohr Academy is to offer a quality education while providing an extended family atmosphere for students, families, and faculty. Younger and older students are offered many opportunities to work together throughout the school day. Family participation is encouraged in classroom activities and travel opportunities. It is the intention of the Academy to individualize instruction so that each child can progress at his/her own rate. Each child is encouraged and stimulated to develop independent, creative thinking and problem-solving skills. With positive reinforcement offered in daily activities, each child has varied opportunities for success.

An outstanding performing arts program far beyond what is typically expected of schools within the age-range of Academy students makes JRA different from other schools. Students greatly gain from on-stage performing experiences, which compliment and enhance what they learn from a textbook. They learn responsibility, self-confidence and develop a positive self-image through successful performing experiences.

The founders of the Academy have always believed that all students are gifted and talented. Therefore, in addition to reading, language arts, math, science, and social studies, daily classes in computer technology, Spanish, art, music, and physical education give students many opportunities for faculty to help students develop their gifts and talents. In addition, an outstanding enrichment program offers opportunities for experiential learning and character building through varied day-long to week-long field trips, sports teams, and community service activities. Through these activities, students become poised, disciplined, expressive and confident.

Julie Rohr Academy is accredited through the Florida Council of Independent Schools and the Florida Kindergarten Council.

Julie Rohr Academy is a school where mutual respect among teachers, students and parents is fostered. By working together, the Academy can offer a school experience the way it should be in these formative years—fun, creative, motivating and challenging!

SAINT STEPHEN'S EPISCOPAL SCHOOL

ESTABLISHED 1970 **www.saintstephens.org**

Since 1970, Saint Stephen's Episcopal School has been welcoming families of all faiths to its independent day school for students in Pre-Kindergarten 3 through grade 12. Founded by a group of community leaders from Manatee and Sarasota counties, the School now encompasses 35 acres in the heart of Bradenton, Florida and currently serves over 800 students. "A college preparatory curriculum with integrity" best describes the academic program at Saint Stephen's, and includes outstanding athletic and fine arts opportunities for students of all ages.

The School's first Headmaster was the Reverend Rodman Kypke (1970–1971) and the entire student body numbered only 198 students in Kindergarten through eighth grade. Over the next four years, a new grade was added annually and included children from both Manatee and Sarasota Counties. It was during the headmastership of the Reverend Louis Hayden, Jr. (1971–1976) that the now traditional graduation ceremony at Christ Episcopal Church began, when in 1975 the first graduating class of 11 seniors proudly received their diplomas.

A dedicated educator, the Reverend Bennett H. Barnes was appointed Headmaster in 1976. The Upper School enrollment doubled and "new" technology in the form of computers

became a common sight in all divisions. John Howard served as Headmaster from 1987 to 2003. Due to his vision and leadership, numerous advances in programs and upgrading of the campus facilities were implemented over the course of 16 years. The School enjoyed tremendous growth in its student enrollment during this time. A highly-anticipated Pre-Kindergarten program for four-year-olds was born in 1988 adding a new dimension to the Lower School. In 1995, many of the original founders and past members of the Board of Trustees joined together to purchase seven acres for the athletic fields. Another five acres of adjacent land known as the Eckerd Plaza was acquired in 1999, bringing the total campus land area to 35 naturally-wooded acres, and by 2000, the Saint Stephen's family had grown to 684 students. To maintain small class sizes and provide up-to-date learning

facilities, the largest capital campaign in the 30-year history of the school was launched to build a core-complex of three new Upper School buildings. In total, 60,000 square feet of new, enhanced learning facilities were added to the campus.

Jan Pullen became the new Head of School in 2003. She brings a fresh leadership style and new ideas combined with 17 years of Saint Stephen's experience as an administrator and parent. Under her guidance the School has continued to grow and prosper while maintaining its small class size and signature nurturing environment.

The School is fortunate to have direct access to the Manatee River via the McLewis Bayou, which runs through the School's property. In January 2007, thanks to the generous support of the School's community of parents and local business groups, the Upper School's Marine Science classes embarked on their first "on the water" field trip from Saint Stephen's brand-new dock. In years to come students in all divisions will have the opportunity to explore the wonders of Marine and Environmental Science directly from the School's backyard.

The School's emphasis on learning "outside of the classroom" is also represented with its emphasis of sports and physical fitness. All students participate in weekly courses of physical education, and interscholastic sports begins in the Middle School. The campus currently hosts ten practice tennis courts, a practice soccer pitch and regulation soccer pitch, baseball and softball diamonds, and recreational playgrounds for the Lower and Intermediate division students.

With improved facilities has come an increased demand for the type of rigorous education provided by caring and

committed teachers in a small classroom setting. The faculty and administration take great care to preserve the sense of community which is a hallmark of a Saint Stephen's education. The development of the School's excellent elementary academic program and secondary college preparatory curriculum has proven effective over time; Saint Stephen's students continue to excel in academics, with standardized test scores at or above the independent school norms and SAT scores consistently exceeding local, state and national test scores.

The School also offers a thorough Advanced Placement program of courses in the Upper School.

To complement Saint Stephen's academic program, the School's extensive extra-curricular activities, including outstanding athletic, fine arts, and community service opportunities, help students explore their talents and extend their abilities as far as their imaginations and ambitions will take them. Weekly student-led chapels allow students to share and explore their faith in a safe, nurturing environment.

The unique traditions and standards of excellence that embody a Saint Stephen's education remain as strong today as they were when first visualized by the founders of 1970: students who are well prepared for college through a rigorous academic program, and well prepared for a life of service for the greater good, with strong moral values of integrity, responsibility and respect.

The Mission of Saint Stephen's Episcopal School

Provide a superior academic program which prepares each student for a college or university compatible with the individual's academic ability, interest and needs; instill in each student a love of learning, an active respect for all members of the School community, and a fundamental sense of integrity; provide a nurturing environment which values self-worth, physical health, spiritual awareness, and responsible citizenship.

THE OUT-OF-DOOR ACADEMY

ESTABLISHED 1924 **www.oda.edu**

Your Child. One Future.

The choice you make for your child's education is critically important for his or her future. Recognized as a Cum Laude School, The Out-of-Door Academy ranks among the top one percent of schools nationwide. With an exceptional focus on academics, students scored among the top five schools in the state of Florida in both SAT scores and Advancement Placement test. 100 percent of graduates have matriculated to a four-year college or university. Along with its premier academic learning environment, students benefit from extraordinary arts and athletics programs. The Out-of-Door Academy provides a caring community for your child, building character and citizenship. They serve more than 600 students in the greater Sarasota-Manatee region from Pre-Kindergarten through Grade 12. As you choose the best path for your child, consider The Out-of-Door Academy. At Out-of-Door, children develop to their full potential and graduate prepared for an outstanding future.

Selby Botanical Gardens, G.WIZ, The Hands-On Science Museum, Sarasota Jungle Gardens and various area colleges.

An indication of how much the area supports its schools is that each of the elementary, middle, high schools and charter schools has a School Advisory Council (SAC) composed of parents, teachers and administrators. In addition, the school system can point to 19,000 volunteers, including students, adults, senior citizens and business leaders who participate in (PALs) Partner in Education Programs. Offering students and teachers their expertise and talent, they are an invaluable resource for the whole county school system.

The results speak for themselves. Sarasota County consistently ranks among the top school systems in Florida. In 2006, 4th graders were ranked #1 among the 67 county school districts in the state in the writing portion of the Florida Comprehensive Assessment Test (FCAT). Indeed, students at all grade levels where the FCATs are administered perform above the state average. During the 2003-04 school year, seniors who took the SAT scored 63 points higher than other state students and 35 points higher than their national peers.

There are also 29 state-registered private schools in the area, including the Out-of-Door Academy on Siesta Key, New Gate School, which provides Montessori education for elementary and secondary students, Cardinal Mooney High School and Julie Rohr Academy, to name a few. St. Stephens Episcopal School in Bradenton attracts students from all over the world.

COLLEGES AND UNIVERSITIES

While higher education may have taken a backseat to the arts in Sarasota in the past, that is no longer the case. The area is now home to nine colleges and universities, two of them with national and international reputations.

New College, an undergraduate liberal arts school, is the honors college in the Florida State University system. Flanking both sides of U.S. 41 by the Sarasota-Bradenton International Airport, its scenic campus occupies the former Edith and Charles Ringling estate. Originally founded by local civic leaders as a private institution for gifted students, it has always had a reputation for an innovative and experimental approach to higher education. With 70 faculty members, a 10:1

Youth activities create social interaction and teach acceptance among different ethic groups.

ratio of students to faculty and small classes, the school values individuality, freedom, self-motivation and excellence. Students design their own curriculum, sign learning contracts and receive written evaluations at the end of the semester. In 2007, *The Princeton Review* rated New College the best value in public education, and it tied for first place in the *US News and World Report* ranking of public liberal arts colleges. Alumni include physicists, musicians, mathematicians, CEOs, physicians, lawyers, college professors and presidents, as well as a U.S. Congressman.

A mile to the south lies the Ringling College of Art and Design, one of the premier elite fine arts schools in the United States. The institution, which was founded by circus impresario John Ringling, attracts students from all over the world. Located on a picturesque 35-acre campus, it serves close to 1,100 students from 43 states and 23 foreign countries. Following in the footsteps of its visionary founder, the school celebrates innovation and cutting-edge technology. As an early proponent of "the computer as the paint brush of the future," it has built renowned programs of computer animation. In recent decades, there is scarcely a Hollywood animated or special effects movie on which Ringling graduates have not worked. In addition, alumni are prominent in the computer gaming industry, advertising and automobile design, as well as in sculpture, painting and graphic arts.

After sharing its campus with New College for more than thirty years, the University of South Florida (USF) Sarasota-Manatee recently occupied a brand new campus at the historic Crosley Mansion north of the airport. Providing junior and senior level courses for 28 bachelor's degrees, as well as 11 master's degrees, USF Sarasota-Manatee serves more than 3,200 students. Many of the programs have been developed with the advice of a Community Leadership Council made up of 42 business leaders from the Sarasota-Bradenton area. As a result, the school offers highly successful programs in criminal justice administration, nursing informatics (dealing with management information systems in patient care), and hotel and restaurant management.

In recent years, there have been efforts to capitalize on the concentration in one geographic locale of cultural and educational institutions—the Ringling College of Art and Design, New College, USF Sarasota-Manatee and The Florida State University Ringling Center for the

Cultural Arts—to literally and figuratively "put the area on the map." The result has been an exciting initiative called Innovation 41. The idea is to create a gateway corridor to the regions cultural and educational resources along the North Tamiami Trail from downtown Sarasota to southern Manatee County. The study begun in 2005 has sought input from over 300 participants—business owners, residents, students, faculty, administrators and government officials. A consultant team has prepared a master plan that addresses overall visual appearance, transportation issues and ways to integrate the various institutions into a cohesive whole to give the corridor a unique identity and unified character.

In 1957, the Florida Legislature awarded a charter to the (then) Manatee Junior College, the two-year community college that became the area's first public institution of higher learning. Its beginnings were humble—502 students meeting in borrowed space. Now, 50 years later, Manatee Community College (MCC) serves over 9,000 credit students and 21,000 residents taking non-credit classes in a wide variety of subjects. The school has two 100-acre campuses in Bradenton and Venice, the Center for Innovation and Technology in Lakewood Ranch, and a host of online classes. More than 50 percent of college-bound high school students in Sarasota and Manatee Counties go to MCC each year, and the school is among the top 100 granting associate degrees each year.

Lakewood Ranch, the planned super community east of I-75, has become home to a number of important institutions of higher learning. The Sarasota branch of Keiser University, a private institution with 12 campuses throughout Florida, occupies a three-story building just off University Parkway. The school offers associate and bachelor's degrees, as well as continuing education in professional and job-related training. The focus is career-oriented in areas such as elementary education, health services administration, nursing, criminal justice, business administration and computer programming. Keiser University's Capital Culinary Institute offers the only associate degree program in the culinary arts on the West Coast of Florida.

The building next door houses the Sarasota branch of Everglades University, which offers bachelor's and master's degrees in aviation technology and management, alternative medicine, business administration and construction management. A concentrated approach,

Young and talented minds exploring science.

NEW COLLEGE OF FLORIDA

ESTABLISHED 1960 **www.ncf.edu**

New College of Florida is a national leader in undergraduate liberal arts education. Located on a 110-acre campus on Sarasota Bay, the public honors college attracts highly-motivated, academically-talented students from throughout the United States and abroad.

New College's intimate environment, consisting of nearly 800 students and more than 70 faculty members, allows for in-depth undergraduate research and personalized learning. With a student/faculty ratio of 10:1, students work collaboratively with their faculty on coursework, research and independent study projects, both on campus and in locations around the world. A record number of Fulbright Scholars for an institution of its size is one earmark of the college's rigorous academic standards. *U.S. News & World Report* has ranked New College the #1 public liberal arts college

in the nation, and it is one of only 40 colleges nationwide to be featured in Loren Pope's book, *Colleges That Change Lives*.

New College is the #2 public college/university in the nation for sending graduates on to elite law, medical and business schools, according to *The Wall Street Journal*. New College alumni are the leaders in their fields. Among them are Fields Medal winner and mathematician William Thurston, national news correspondent Alexis Simendinger and Chatham University President Esther Barazzone.

Since its founding in 1960, New College has been an integral part of the Sarasota community. The Sarasota Reading Festival evolved out of the New College Reading Festival, and the renowned Sarasota Music Festival began in 1965 as the New College Music Festival. The College has won service awards from the NAACP, the YMCA and

Sarasota County government. New College plays a vital role in Sarasota's arts and social scene with a contemporary music series called New Music New College and the Library Association's elegant Mistletoe Ball.

The future looks bright for New College of Florida. Under the leadership of President Gordon E. "Mike" Michalson, the College completed a visionary master plan that incorporates state-of-the-art environmental design into campus architecture and landscaping, thus playing a key role in the transformation of the North Trail in Sarasota over the next 25 years.

UNIVERSITY OF SOUTH FLORIDA
SARASOTA-MANATEE

ESTABLISHED 1974 **www.sarasota.usf.edu**

Hometown Campus.
National Prestige.

The University of South Florida Sarasota-Manatee is an upper-level, regional campus of the University of South Florida (USF), the ninth-largest public university in the nation and a top-tier research university as classified by the Carnegie Foundation.

USF Sarasota-Manatee opened in 1974 as the southernmost campus of the University of South Florida. Today, the campus offers over 40 bachelor's degree, master's degree, and certificate programs to college students who have earned at least 60 hours of transferable credits.

In keeping with the vision of the university, USF Sarasota-Manatee's academic programs are aligned with the local community's business, economic and workforce needs. The campus offers strong curricula in business, criminology, education, hospitality management, information technology, nursing, social work, engineering, and the liberal arts.

The local campus prides itself in preparing professionals in high-demand fields for the needs of a rapidly-changing world.

The university is accredited by the nationally recognized Southern Association of Colleges and Schools (SACS). Many prestigious, specialized accreditors have also recognized the academic quality of USF by awarding professional accreditation in teacher education, educational leadership, business administration, engineering, nursing, rehabilitation and mental health counseling, social work, public administration, and other professions.

Graduates of the accounting program are consistently among the highest scorers in the nation on the Certified Public Accountant (CPA) exam. Master's degree programs in education consistently rank among the top-rated by *U.S. News & World Report*.

Along with exceptionally strong academic programs and the prestige and resources of the University of South Florida, USF Sarasota-Manatee offers its students a friendly, hometown campus setting, small class sizes that average 16 students, and individualized faculty attention.

Flexible scheduling and affordable tuition allow students of all ages to balance family, work, and college course work. Students choose from course offerings during the morning, mid-day, evening, and weekend, as well as online. Notably, USF's tuition is among the lowest in the region, and the campus offers supportive financial aid and scholarship opportunities. On-campus childcare and dining services add to student convenience.

Many local Manatee Community College students participate in a "2 + 2" program, and make an easy transition to

bachelor's degree programs after completing their two-year associate's degrees. They enroll at MCC for their first two years (freshman & sophomore), and then at USF for their third and fourth years (junior & senior). USF Sarasota-Manatee also has a seamless articulation agreement for graduates of select associate's degree programs at Keiser University to assist them in earning their bachelor's degrees.

Students and the local community alike enjoy a unique opportunity provided by the Institute for Public Policy & Leadership. The program helps shape the future social, economic, and governmental environments that influence the lives of citizens, especially in the South Tampa Bay region, by serving as an effective, high quality knowledge resource, broker and facilitator.

The Academy for Lifelong Learning, an affiliate of the Elderhostel Institute Network, provides a continuous peer teaching/learning experience rich with social interactions and opportunities for adults who would like noncredit courses for personal interest.

With a student body of more than 3,500 annually, the campus attracts outstanding people of all ages from across the region. The average student is 32 years old, but the student body ranges in age from 18 to 84. Nearly 75% of the students work, with about half working full-time.

Nestled behind a nature preserve on North Tamiami Trail (US 41) along beautiful Sarasota Bay, the brand new USF Sarasota-Manatee campus building is a 100,000 square foot state-of-the-art, Mediterranean-style structure inspired by beautiful historic mansions in the area. The facility offers 26 classrooms, an auditorium, seminar and video-conferencing rooms, computer labs, a childcare center, dining facility, student gathering places, faculty and staff offices, and a technology and learning center.

Impressive arrays of high-tech learning tools are wired into the new building, making it a technology showcase for the convergence of voice, video, and data. All 26 classrooms are fully outfitted with the latest instructional technologies for complete audio/video integration into each teaching station, setting the highest standards for "smart" classrooms.

In addition to its main location in Sarasota on US 41 across from the Sarasota-Bradenton International Airport, USF Sarasota-Manatee boasts a location in south Sarasota county on South Tamiami Trail (US 41) at Manatee Community College in Venice.

RINGLING COLLEGE OF ART AND DESIGN

ESTABLISHED 1931 **www.ringling.edu**

Founded in 1931, by noted art collector, real estate magnate, and circus impresario, John Ringling and integral to Sarasota's growing cultural mosaic is Ringling College of Art and Design, a breeding ground for some of the world's most talented artists and designers. This private, independent, four-year College has grown into one of the most prestigious institutions of its kind in the nation alongside the Rhode Island School of Design, Pratt Institute, Parsons School of Design, and the Art Institute of Chicago.

In 2006, *BusinessWeek* recognized Ringling as one of top design schools in the world, and in 2007, the acclaimed *3D World* magazine, named the college's Computer Animation program #1 in North America. Ringling is also noted as one of the most technologically advanced art

colleges with a computer to student ratio of better than 1:2—rivaling that of M.I.T.

Nearly 1,200 students from around the globe pursue their Bachelor of Fine Arts degrees in one of 13 programs: Advertising Design, Broadcast Design/Motion Graphics, Computer Animation, Digital Film, Fine Arts, Game Art & Design, Graphic & Interactive Communication, Illustration, Interior Design, Painting, Printmaking, Photography & Digital Imaging and Sculpture.

An innovative Bachelor of Arts degree in the Business of Art & Design combines a well-rounded education in the arts and creative problem solving with essential business skills so necessary in today's global economy.

Beyond study in their chosen art and design discipline, students benefit from a dynamic and well-rounded liberal arts education and the personal attention of 130 dedicated faculty members, all practicing artists, designers, and scholars, who bring their professional expertise into the classroom further enhancing students' career preparedness.

With deep ties to the creative industries, each year nearly 50 recruiters from top companies visit the Ringling College campus to hire its students. These organizations include such notable names as Apple, Disney, Hallmark Cards, Electronic Arts, DreamWorks, Pixar, Target, the C.I.A., and Sony Pictures ImageWorks who chose the College as one of only six schools in its inaugural IPAX program.

There are numerous art exhibits to capture the imagination.

combining small classes on campus and online, allows students to complete master's degree programs in as little as a 14 months.

The Lake Erie College of Osteopathic Medicine (LECOM) opened its satellite branch in Bradenton in 2004 with 150 students. The four-year medical school has a faculty of 30 full-time and more than 200 adjunct physicians and is the fastest growing medical college in the United States. The school trains physicians and pharmacists in innovative, problem-based learning courses. Doctors of osteopathic medicine (D.O.s) are just like M.D.s, but they have additional training in musculoskeletal manipulation, and their ranks are growing in leaps and bounds. Although D.O.s comprise only six percent of doctors in the United States, they represent 21 percent of medical students. By the time LECOM graduates its first class in 2008, it will have its full complement of 600 students.

Argosy University/Sarasota is located at the intersection of Honore and 17th Streets in northeastern Sarasota. The private school, one of 18 campuses throughout the United States, offers undergraduate, master's and doctorate degrees in the areas of business, education and psychology. Working professionals can further their education while continuing their career by means of an innovative distance learning model that combines intense one-week residency instruction with online study and off-site tutorials. Webster University's Sarasota/Manatee campus opened in 2000 to assist career-minded professionals in pursuing graduate studies. Located on Cooper Creek Boulevard north of University Parkway, it offers master's degree programs in counseling, human resources, management and leadership, and business administration for students who hold a bachelor's degree from a regionally accredited college or university.

OTHER EDUCATIONAL RESOURCES

In addition to the public and private school systems, Sarasota has a wealth of other educational resources. Many of the arts organizations have schools for youths and adults, offering courses, workshops and camps throughout the regular school year and during the summer. Notable among them are the Asolo Repertory Theatre, The Players and The Florida Ballet. Florida Studio Theatre has an extensive school wing, as well as its Write-A-Play program, which tours Florida schools and encourages children of all ages to write short plays and submit them to the theater. Winning entries receive performances by professional actors during the Young Playwrights Festival in May.

The Sarasota County Arts Council's Artists-in-Schools program brings professional artists into schools through performances, lectures, workshops, master classes and multi-disciplinary projects. The program also includes events in other venues such as parks, hospitals, community centers, correctional facilities and businesses.

In its Center for School & Public Programs, Mote Marine Laboratory presents on-site learning experiences for schools, families and other professional and social organizations throughout the year. Teams of scientist-educators also provide in-depth learning experiences for teachers, students and visitors during summer camps. G.WIZ, The Hands-On Science Museum, located close to downtown Sarasota next to the Van Wezel Performing Arts Hall, offers fun programs throughout the year to individuals and groups from public and private schools, social service agencies and community organizations. Many exhibits illustrate scientific principles and invite the participation of visitors.

The Sarasota County Library System has eight locations throughout the county. Selby Library, the main branch downtown, has a beautiful marine exhibit, a large curved fish tank that serves as the portal to the children's section. Selby also houses the Sarasota Music Archive, one of the leading music reference collections in the United States, containing several hundred thousand recordings, tapes, sheet music, books, vinyl record, CDs and Edison wax cylinders. There are also special collections for Florida genealogy, gardening and grant research. And the Community Video Archives, established in 1991, documents and preserves living history of the county in biographic and thematic videos.

health

health

WHEN PEOPLE CONSIDER THE QUALITY OF LIFE of a region, health and medical care are often uppermost on their minds. In the case of Sarasota County and its neighbor to the north, Manatee County, both visitors and residents can be assured that they are being served by one of the most progressive and well-respected hospital and physician networks in the nation. Whether it is neonatal or geriatric care, heart disease or cancer treatment,

mental health or addiction services, the region has a history of outstanding facilities and physicians. Area hospitals consistently rank among the best hospitals in the nation both in specific categories and general patient care. With nine area hospitals and rehabilitation centers, employing nearly 9,000, the health care industry is also a vital economic component of the region. Sarasota Memorial Health Care System, for example, is the county's second-largest employer. Manatee Memorial Hospital and Manatee Glens rank among the top 15 employers in Manatee County. Taken together, the hospitals also attract and utilize over 3,000 volunteers.

Organized medicine came to the area during the 1920s as a result of the first Florida real estate boom. Faced with a growing need in health care, Sarasota residents began to raise funds for construction of a hospital.

Healthy residents enjoy the endless sunny days Sarasota has to offer.

In 1925, Sarasota Hospital opened with 32 beds and 10 full-time employees. The following year a school for nurses was established. As the facility quickly outgrew its capacity, an annex was added to accommodate patient overflow. By the mid-1930s, what was then called the Sarasota Municipal Hospital had expanded to 100 beds.

More changes and expansion followed both in facilities and services. In 1949, the Florida Legislature created a special hospital district in Sarasota, affirming the hospital's mission as a public, not-for-profit institution. The governor appointed nine local residents to the newly formed Hospital Board, giving people in the community a direct say in medical policy. In 1954, the hospital was deeded to the Board and renamed Sarasota Memorial Hospital in honor of the veterans of both world wars.

The second Florida boom of the 1950s with its unprecedented population explosion increased the demand for medical services throughout the region. As a result, new hospitals were built, one in Venice and two in Bradenton. Sarasota Memorial Hospital underwent massive new construction to expand and modernize the facility. When dedication ceremonies were held for the new south wing in 1955 of the five-story hospital, it became one of the few fully air conditioned facilities in the South.

Since then, it has continued to respond to the growing needs in the community while exploring the most up-to-date medical technologies and procedures. In 1999, Sarasota Memorial Hospital became one of the first hospitals in the nation to use a robotic device in open heart surgery. It was one of the first non-academic hospitals in the nation to develop clinical research services and has conducted almost 200 clinical trials in the last 10 years. Today, it is know as Sarasota Memorial Health Care System.

For the past three years, *US News and World Report* has ranked Sarasota Memorial Health Care System as one of the best in the nation in six categories: heart surgery, orthopedics, cancer care, digestive disorders, gynecology and respiratory disorders. As the second-largest acute-care hospital in Florida, it is among the top 25 hospitals in the U.S. for the number of open heart surgeries and in the top 10 for the number of joint replacements each year. It is also the only hospital in Sarasota County that offers obstetrics and inpatient pediatric care.

The other area hospitals also provide outstanding patient care and various specialized services that have resulted in national recognition.

Doctors Hospital of Sarasota is a general care facility that provides oncology, orthopedic and neurological care, as well as a special wound-care center. In 2005, it opened a new spine Care Center. It is a Joint Commission on Accreditation of Health Care Organizations (JCAHO) certified Primary Stroke Center and is consistently ranked in the 95th percentile nationwide for patient satisfaction.

DATTOLI CANCER CENTER & BRACHYTHERAPY RESEARCH INSTITUTE

ESTABLISHED 2000 www.dattoli.com

The decision to open a world class center for the non-surgical treatment of prostate cancer in Sarasota was easy to make. Sarasota offers so much for the local staff and the international patient base ... year-round sub-tropical climate, convenient regional air transportation, a wealth of recreational and cultural activities, and a hospital which is consistently ranked in the top 50 by USA Today.

In early 2000, Drs. Michael Dattoli and Richard Sorace, with Chief Executive Officer Donald Kaltenbach, set their sights on a driver-friendly location at Fruitville Road and Tuttle Avenue to transform into the most technologically sophisticated free-standing prostate cancer center in the world. Major renovations, including the construction of radiation-tight vaults and the delivery of several million dollars of diagnostic and treatment equipment, preceded the Center's opening.

Since that time, over 5,000 men have come to the Center for true leading edge non-surgical treatment for prostate cancer. The Dattoli protocol includes the newest 4D IG-IMRT (image-guided intensity modulated radiation therapy) with DART (dynamic adaptive radiation therapy), followed by Paladium-103 brachytherapy (seed implant). Long-term results of this successful protocol have been reported in the nation's leading medical journals, including *Cancer*, *Urology* and the *International Journal of Radiation Oncology, Biology and Physics*. A better than 90% cure rate, even for men with advanced cancers, is setting the standard at the Dattoli Cancer Center.

The Dattoli Cancer Center employs 35, and houses the non-profit Dattoli Cancer Foundation. Patients are treated 6 AM to 7 PM daily, utilizing two Varian linear accelerators. The Center saw the first installation of the Varian equipment. This pioneering system is upgraded annually. Other special equipment includes 3D Color-Flow Doppler Ultrasound, a high-speed helical GE CT Scanner with QCT application and a suite of Varis planning computers.

The Center's mission is to provide each patient with his best chance for cure while eliminating or limiting the negative side effects of treatment. A comprehensive patient education program, including weekly seminars and an award-winning patient handbook round out the treatment experience for patients and family members.

The Center's research initiative insures that progress continues in finding better diagnostic and treatment options. Dr. Dattoli's international speaking engagements share the excitement of these successes.

It is no wonder that men from all over the world find their way to Sarasota for treatment at the Dattoli Cancer Center. Their successful treatment here serves as the best advertising possible—word of mouth.

SARASOTA MEMORIAL
HEALTH CARE SYSTEM

ESTABLISHED 1925 **www.smh.com**

Legend has it that the women who raised funds to build the community's first modern hospital were so determined that no businessman dared venture down Main Street without pulling his pockets inside out to make a public declaration he had no more money to give the hospital fund.

It was the early 1920s and the temporary "tent hospital" and six-bed facility used to treat patients was simply no longer adequate. Working tirelessly, these extraordinary women raised $40,000 to build the county's first hospital. On November 2, 1925, with hundreds of residents in attendance, Sarasota Hospital opened its doors.

Today, that modest 32-bed facility run by the county's welfare association has grown

into the Sarasota Memorial Health Care System, a regional referral center with an 806-bed hospital, long and short-term skilled nursing center, home health services, walk-in urgent care centers, laboratory and imaging centers and specialty campuses stretching across the region.

But even more impressive than the breadth of services offered is

the list in even a single category. Sarasota Memorial placed among the best in six: heart care and heart surgery, cancer care, ortho-pedics, gynecology, respiratory disorders, and digestive disorders.

As testimony to the hospital's success, the former head of the National Red Cross and the National Institutes of Health, Bernadine Healy, MD, singled out Sarasota Memorial on CNN as an example of how patients can find superior care in their own community. In responding to a question about whether people who did not live near top-ranked

"The hospital, which was the dream of many, was made possible by the intensive efforts of a few and the generosity of all." —*SARASOTA HERALD*, NOV. 2, 1925

the quality of care Sarasota Memorial provides. In its yearly study of nearly 6,000 institutions nationwide, *U.S. News & World Report* determines the best 50 hospitals in 17 different specialties. In 2006, only 176 centers made

teaching institutions still receive "innovative treatment," Healy cited the hospital and its 2006 rankings in six categories as an example of "excellent care," saying "a great tribute to American medicine is the diffusion of excellent quality

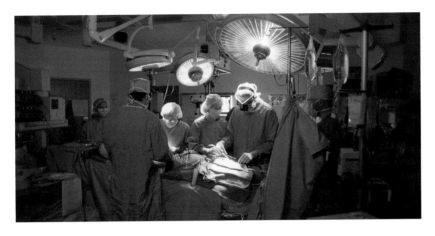

high-risk pregnancies and critically ill newborns, the only hospital with a dedicated Pediatrics Unit and specialists on hand to care for hospitalized children, and the only hospital with a dedicated unit and specialized staff for patients with psychiatric conditions.

Throughout the years, the community support that helped build Sarasota's first modern hospital has continued. Much of the highly specialized equipment and advanced technology has been made possible through community donations, largely through the labors of Sarasota Memorial Healthcare Foundation, Inc. Since 1976, the foundation has contributed more than $31 million, through its mission of *Voluntary Action for the Public Good*, for technological advances like the new da Vinci surgical robot, expanded emergency room services, even special ambulances to transport at-risk heart patients and pregnant women. All this in addition to more than $1 million for the continuing education of doctors and nurses.

Because of Sarasota Memorial's essential role in the community it will continue to grow. In 2007, the hospital began moving forward with plans to build a new multi-million dollar replacement bed-tower, a critical project to relieve overcrowded and aging facilities.

In doing so, Sarasota Memorial will honor its past, continuing the work—and keeping the spirit alive—of those first founding mothers who cared so much for the health of our community.

from major teaching centers into community hospitals."

Indeed, the hospital's heart program has consistently ranked in the top 25 hospitals in the nation—the highest ranked Florida hospital. And with outcomes and mortality rates among the best in the nation, Sarasota Memorial's Institute for Cancer Care has received equal billing.

It is the community's unwavering commitment to high quality care that has helped the hospital attract the nation's best doctors, researchers and nurses. Sarasota Memorial is among just 2 percent of hospitals in the country to earn Magnet status, the highest honor awarded to a nursing program. Awarded by the American Nurses' Credentialing Center, the nation's premiere

authority on nursing, Magnet recognition means the hospital provides a supportive environment that attracts and retains the best caregivers and demonstrates superiority in all facets of care.

Despite its tremendous growth and all its honors, Sarasota County's only publicly owned hospital remains true to its founding mission—to be the safety net of care for the people in this community.

And so it remains the only hospital in the county delivering "mission" services—costly care that other local hospitals have scaled back or eliminated completely. Today, Sarasota Memorial is the only hospital in Sarasota County that delivers babies, the only hospital equipped to care for women with

Venice Regional Medical Center was founded in 1951. The 312-bed facility ranks among the top 100 stroke hospitals in the country. Its orthopedics department has been recognized for its knee replacement and fracture repair services. With specialized cardiac care and accredited cancer services, the hospital serves a large area beyond South County.

Further to the south, Englewood Community Hospital is the only acute care facility in the county accredited by the Society of Chest Pain Centers. It also offers a round-the-clock nurses hotline for patients who have urgent care questions.

Manatee Memorial Hospital in Bradenton was founded in 1953. The 319-bed acute care facility is owned and operated by a subsidiary of Universal Health Services, Inc. One of two hospitals in Manatee County to operate obstetric units, it garnered national recognition in 2007 when it received a five-star, the highest rating in orthopedic and maternity services according to a comprehensive study released by HealthGrades, the nation's leading healthcare ratings company.

Blake Medical Center, also in Manatee County, has been named a Solucient 100 Top Hospital nine times—a designation achieved by only two other hospitals in the U.S. The 383-bed acute care facility opened a Spine Care Center in 2005, and operates a heartburn relief center with the latest testing capabilities.

In 2004, Lakewood Ranch Medical Center opened with 120 beds. Located on a 30-acre medical campus east of I-75 in the Town Center of Lakewood Ranch, the new hospital offers comprehensive medical services, including acute and surgical care. Its radiology department has

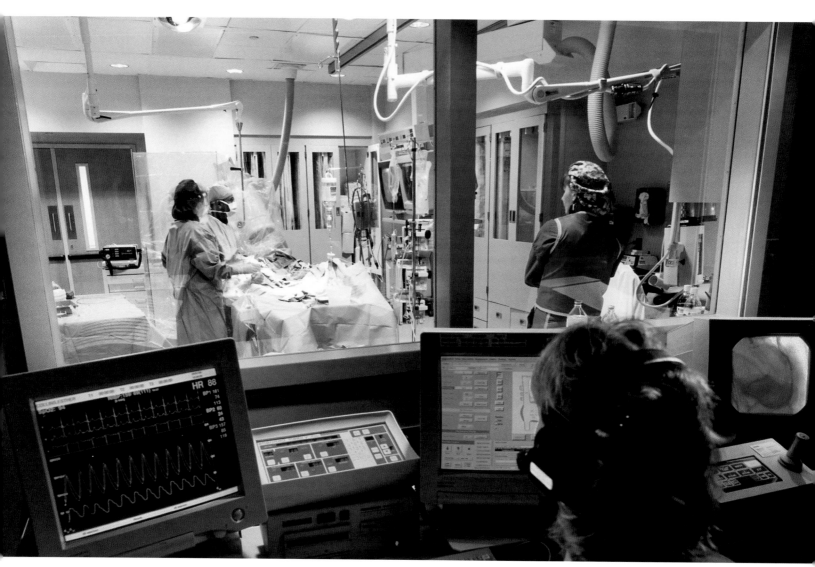

State-of-the-art heath care technology that ensures our public health and well being.

a state-of-the art cardiovascular imaging lab. The hospital also has a Women's Service Center, and its birthing center is the other obstetric unit in Manatee County.

All the above hospitals also provide 24/7 emergency care in ERs and walk-in clinics for life-threatening problems and non-life-threatening conditions that require immediate attention.

Sarasota County also has the only two freestanding rehabilitation hospitals in Southwest Florida, operated by HealthSouth, the largest provider of inpatient rehabilitation in the U.S. HealthSouth Rehabilitation Hospital provides 76 beds and services for stroke, multiple sclerosis, Parkinson's, muscular dystrophy and Lou Gehrig's Disease patients. HealthSouth RidgeLake Hospital has 40 beds and focuses on patients with neurological conditions. HealthSouth also provides comprehensive outpatient services at its main campus and two satellite centers on University Parkway and Bee Ridge Road.

There is also a special care facility for children, the All Children's Specialty Care of Sarasota. An 18,000 square foot outpatient center, it was opened by St. Petersburg's renowned All Children's Hospital in conjunction with Sarasota Memorial Health Care System, and is affiliated with the University of South Florida's College of Medicine. Among its specialties are pediatric speech pathologies, audiology issues, and pediatric physical therapy services.

For mental health services in Sarasota County, Sarasota Memorial Health Care System provides both inpatient and outpatient services.

In Bradenton, Manatee Glens is the community's oldest provider of mental health and addiction services and only one of six mental health care centers in Florida that operates a hospital. Founded more than 50 years ago, it has 450 employees and provides counseling and other services to children, adolescents and adults. Its outpatient detox program has become a role model for other programs in Florida. Manatee Glens also provides outreach and education services to prevent addictions before they begin and offers an employee assistance program for area businesses.

In addition, Manatee Memorial Hospital has a Center for Behavioral Health. And several organizations, such as Samaritan Counseling Services of the Gulf Coast, Coastal Behavioral Healthcare, Charis Center,

Mental Health Community Centers, and Florida Center for Child and Family Development offer counseling and support services.

Sarasota is also home to a number of specialty physicians whose work has garnered national and international attention.

The Dattoli Cancer Center attracts prostate cancer patients from around the world. Dr. Michael Dattoli, a pioneer in the field of prostate brachytherapy, a specialized form of radiation therapy, developed many of the innovations that have become alternative treatments of prostate cancer without surgery. Refining techniques since 1986, the Dattoli Center has built the largest brachytherapy program in the country. Its 13-year monitoring of patients makes it the longest standing and largest study of non-surgical cancer treatment results in the world.

The Radiation Oncology Centers with locations in Sarasota, Venice, Englewood and Port Charlotte, has served the area since 1975. It performed the first prostate seed implant therapy in the area nearly 30 years ago, and continues to participate in the most up-to-date research and development of prostate cancer treatments.

Sarasota's ophthalmologists have been in the forefront of cataract and laser surgery, participating in early clinical trials for new procedures and products of cataract, implant and refractive surgery. In the process, they have helped revolutionize the field. As a result, such doctors as Dr. Harry Grabow of Sarasota Cataract & Laser Institute, Dr. Keye Wong of Sarasota Retina Institute, and Dr. David Shoemaker and Dr. William Lahners of Center for Sight have developed national and international reputations and clientele.

When it comes to aid for the blind and visually impaired, there are several strong organizations in the area, including Lighthouse of Manasota. Southeastern Guide Dogs in Palmetto is a nationally recognized training facility. Since its inception in 1982, it has placed over 2,000 guide dogs in 36 U.S. states and Canada.

Over the last 30 years, the Sarasota area has also become a magnet for alternative medical approaches. There are well-respected acupuncturist physicians and doctors of integrative medicine who combine traditional western practices and oriental and non-traditional medicine. In the new and growing field of anti-aging medicine, Sarasota is home to two of only a thousand board certified doctors. The Sarasota School of Massage Therapy has trained licensed massage therapists since 1978. Additionally, the RoseMary Birthing Home offers water births, home births, aquanatal classes, lactating counseling and postpartum support by licensed midwives.

The tradition of caring for the elderly in Sarasota goes back to the 1940s when concerned citizens recognized a need for a nursing home to cope for a growing population of senior citizens with health issues. The Kiwanis Club took on the responsibility, raised the necessary funds, purchased land on 12th Street and Orange Avenue, and opened the Sarasota Welfare Home in 1948 as a not-for-profit facility overseen by a volunteer board of directors. Renamed The Pines of Sarasota in 1988, the facility has grown to a 13-acre campus with 19 buildings, including a secured Alzheimer's unit. With more than 300 employees, it serves up to 276 residents and 50 day clients.

Throughout Sarasota County, there are now more than 100 high-quality assisted-living facilities and nursing homes, ranging from luxury communities to specialized care places for patients suffering from Alzheimer's disease and neurological disorders.

The Senior Friendship Center with two scenic campuses in Venice and downtown Sarasota was founded in 1973. It is dedicated to relieving the loneliness and isolation many elders experience, while providing free and low-cost health services, adult day care, recreational programs and home meal deliveries.

For end-of-life support and care, the TideWell Hospice and Palliative Care has helped patients and families deal with advanced illness since 1980. Originally tucked away in a two-room office in Sarasota Memorial Hospital, it has since grown into one of the nation's largest not-for-profit hospices, and now operates five hospice houses in four Southwest Florida counties, serving more than 6,000 patients each year.

As people continue to flock to Southwest Florida, area hospitals, physicians and support institutions continue to expand to meet the growing demand for high-quality medical services. Some of the established hospitals are opening satellite branches and outpatient facilities throughout the county. Mobile clinics are exploring ways to provide services in neighborhoods. There are also plans to build a brand new hospital in North Port, Sarasota County's fastest growing city.

arts

arts &
culture

FOR OVER 80 YEARS SARASOTA HAS BEEN A
cultural magnet attracting architects,
musicians, artists and writers. No other
community this size in the world can
boast a cultural scene of such density and
variety. The area includes three professional theaters, four community theaters,
opera and ballet companies, a symphony
orchestra, a large performing hall, an elite
art school and a world-class art museum.

There are also numerous art, music and film festivals throughout the year, which enhance the area's national and international art reputation. No wonder Sarasota is known as the Cultural Capital of Florida.

It all began during the first Florida boom when two visionary developers brought the arts to town. A.B. Edwards, Sarasota's first mayor, built a three-story theater on the corner of First Street and Pineapple. Designed in the popular Mediterranean Revival style of the time, it opened in 1926 and presented musicals, operas, silent movies and vaudeville productions. Over the decades, it saw the likes of W.C. Fields, Will Rogers and Elvis Presley, as well as movie premieres such as *The Yearling* and Cecil B. DeMille's *The Greatest Show on Earth*. The building now houses the Sarasota Opera and has become one of the anchors for downtown's theater district.

Solarium in the Cà d'Zan mansion, the Ringlings' winter home.

The same year three miles to the north, John Ringling, the great circus showman, built a palatial waterfront home for his wife Mable. He named the 30-room mansion Cà d'Zan—the name means "John's house" in an obscure Italian dialect—and held lavish parties on the terrace overlooking the bay. Built in the style of a Mediterranean palazzo right on the water, it has been fully restored, and is now a museum in its own right and one of the main attractions on the large estate, housing tapestries and carved gilded furniture.

In 1927, Ringling also built a museum on his estate to house his extensive collection of Renaissance and Baroque paintings. After his death in 1936, the State of Florida took ownership and turned it into a museum complex. Now affiliated with Florida State University (FSU), the John and Mable Ringling Museum is the largest museum/university complex in the United States, and displays such masters as Rubens, Velasquez and El Greco, as well as American and contemporary paintings, Asian Art and traveling exhibitions.

In addition to the art museum, the lovely 66-acre estate, filled with exotic banyan trees and a rose garden, is home to a Circus Museum, which displays historical circus artifacts and the largest miniature circus in the world. There is also an information pavilion that houses the Historic Asolo Theater. Created in Asolo, Italy, in 1798 it was purchased and brought to Sarasota in the early 1950s. After housing the Asolo Theater Company and the beginnings of the Sarasota Opera, it fell into disuse. Now lovingly restored, it is America's only 18th century European theater and used for lectures and diverse musical and theatrical events.

Across from the pavilion, a large contemporary edifice—the FSU Center for the Performing Arts—is home to the Asolo Repertory Theatre, the FSU/Asolo Conservatory, one of America's premiere actor training programs, and the Sarasota Ballet of Florida. The building contains two theaters, rehearsal spaces and administrative offices. The 500-seat main stage was modeled on a late 19th century opera house in Dunfermline, Scotland, one of Sarasota's sister cities.

But John Ringling's impact on the arts extended beyond his home. He endowed what is now the Ringling College of Art and Design, attracting talented artists and faculty members to the area. Located about a mile south of the estate, on the Tamiami Trail, the school opened its doors in 1931 with a class of 75 students. The 13-member faculty included Dr. Laura Ganno-McNeill, the first woman in the United States to earn a Ph.D., and Hilton Leech, a prominent watercolorist.

Today, the school is one of the premier art and design training institutions in the world, known for its innovative programs and its leadership in the use of technology in the arts. Its 1,100 students come from all over the U.S. and 23 foreign countries to study Computer Animation, Fine Arts, Digital Film, and Game Art & Design. The scenic 35-acre campus has 90 buildings, including the Selby Gallery, which is open to the public, and is one of Sarasota's foremost galleries for contemporary art.

Although the 1930s and the Great Depression slowed growth in the area to a crawl, there were some bright spots for the arts. The Sarasota Art Association, now Art Center Sarasota, was founded to promote the appreciation of art in the city. And The Players, an amateur theater group, got its start in an abandoned Siesta Golf Club caddie house. One of the oldest community theaters in the county, it now has a home on the North Trail and features a season of musicals in its 300-seat theater.

FLORIDA WEST COAST SYMPHONY

ESTABLISHED 1948 **www.fwcs.org**

Experience the Power of Music

Located in the heart of Sarasota, the Beatrice Friedman Symphony Center is home to the 450-seat Holley Hall and the Florida West Coast Symphony. The hallmark 60th anniversary in 2008/2009 extends the Symphony's record as the oldest continuing orchestra in the state of Florida. A multi-faceted organization, the Symphony is deeply committed to both performance and educational excellence.

Entertainment for All

With a performance schedule of nearly 100 concerts in its September through May season, the Symphony boasts programs that appeal to all music lovers. Repertoire includes everything from masterwork compositions and chamber music to light classics and popular favorites. The extraordinary talent of guest artists frequently garnishes that of the full professional orchestra, led by Maestro Leif Bjaland.

Home to the Sarasota Music Festival

The Symphony's educational programs cater to enthusiastic students of all ages and abilities. In addition to traditional music lessons, group classes and community outreach programs, the Symphony is the parent organization of the prestigious Sarasota Music Festival. Held each June, the Sarasota Music Festival welcomes world renowned music masters who serve as the faculty for the 85 advanced music students, selected from nearly 500 applicants, who come from around the globe to study and perform in Sarasota. The Festival includes nine concerts featuring the faculty musicians and several free student concerts—all are open to the public.

Performance Venues and Contact

For more information about the Florida West Coast Symphony, directions to a performance venue, concert schedules or to purchase tickets online, you will find their website to be all inclusive.

The hallmark 60th anniversary in 2008/2009 extends the Symphony's record as the oldest continuing orchestra in the state of Florida.

THE JOHN AND MABLE RINGLING MUSEUM OF ART

ESTABLISHED 1927 **www.ringling.org**

A Must See in Sarasota

The John and Mable Ringling Museum of Art is the remarkable legacy of circus entrepreneur, collector of art and financier John Ringling and his wife Mable. The 66-acre estate includes the Museum of Art's internationally praised collection of European, American and Asian art; the Venetian-Gothic *Cà d'Zan* mansion, winter residence of John and Mable Ringling; the 18th century Historic Asolo Theater; manicured grounds and gardens and the Circus Museum, including the home of the world's largest miniature circus at the Tibbals Learning Center.

A Legacy

Born in poverty but blessed with entrepreneurial genius and spirit, John Ringling (1866-1936) lived the great American success story. For the world, he and his brothers produced *The Greatest Show on Earth*. For the people of Florida, he and his beloved wife, Mable (1875-1929), created their greatest passion, The John and Mable Ringling Museum of Art.

Upon his death in 1936, John Ringling left his art collection and estate to the State of Florida. In 2000, the State of Florida transferred stewardship of the Ringling Museum to Florida State University, establishing the Ringling estate as one of the largest museum/university complexes in the nation.

A Passion for Art

European travel had kindled in the Ringlings a passion for art. John Ringling sought out the advice of savvy art dealers and purchased masterpieces by Rubens, van Dyck, Titian, Velázquez, El Greco, Gainsborough and Reynolds. Among other fine works, Ringling acquired a collection of Cypriot antiquities purchased from the Metropolitan Museum of Art. He dreamed of building his own museum for his treasures. It would be a museum that would emulate the footprint of Florence's Uffizi Gallery, echoing its graceful colonnades and opening onto an Italianate garden. In October 1931, "The John and Mable Ringling Museum of Art" was officially dedicated and opened to the public.

Today, the art collection is enjoyed by visitors from around the world. The Old Master paintings, which are among the rarest and most celebrated in the United States, are the most important of the Museum's holdings. A variety of world-renowned traveling exhibitions are featured year-round in The Ulla R. and Arthur F. Searing Wing.

A Lasting Love Letter

Having traveled often to Europe in search of circus acts, John and Mable came to appreciate the finer pleasures of culture and the exotic treasures of the continent's dazzling architecture. They fell in love with the romance of Venice, and determined that their home Cà d'Zan on Sarasota Bay would match the grandeur of the Doge's Palace, combined with the gothic grace of the Cà d'Oro. Sarasota Bay would become their Grand Canal. The mansion was completed in 1926, and would soon become the epicenter of cultural life on Florida's West Coast, attracting such luminaries as New York Mayor Jimmy Walker, entertainer Flo Ziegfeld, comedian Will Rogers and many others. Lavish parties were held into the morning hours with orchestras serenading guests from the Ringling yacht moored a few feet off the marble terrace. Their dream, to be known through Venetian dialect as the "House of John," became what a later writer would christen John's "love letter to Mable."

A Wonderful Delight

Established in 1948, the Ringling Museum of the American Circus was the first museum of its kind to document the rich history of the circus. With so many circus people living in the immediate area, the collection grew quickly. Because of this, the Ringling Museum has a fine collection including rare handbills and art prints, circus paper, business records, wardrobe, performing props, as well as all types of circus equipment, including beautifully carved parade wagons, sturdy utility wagons, tent poles and massive bail rings.

The Howard Bros. Circus model is an authentic replica of *Ringling Bros. and Barnum & Bailey Circus* when the tented circus was at its largest (circa 1919-1938). Complete with eight main tents, 152 wagons, 1,300 circus performers and workers, more than 800 animals and a 57-car train, the model is a scale replica and occupies 3,800 square feet in the Circus Museum's Tibbals Learning Center. The "largest miniature circus in the world" was created over 50 years by master model builder and philanthropist Howard Tibbals.

A Jewel Box of a Theater

The Historic Asolo Theater is thought to be the only 18th century theater in America. It was originally built in 1798 by architect Antonio Locateli who designed the theater in the Castle of Caterina Cornaro in the Italian town of Asolo near Venice.

The theater was purchased by the Ringling Museum's first director, A. Everett Austin, Jr. and installed on Museum property in the 1950's. This was an era when opera and music performances helped distinguish Sarasota as one of the nation's leading cultural centers. In 2004, the theater was dismantled and in 2006 it was cleaned and prepped for its new home in the Museum's Visitors Pavilion. Today it makes available a diverse roster of theater, dance, music, film and spoken word programs.

Following World War II, another building boom along with air-conditioning allowed the arts to flourish in Sarasota as never before. By the 1950s, Sarasota could boast a thriving visual arts community. Watercolorist Hilton Leech and his wife Dorothy, Thornton Utz, Syd Salomon, Ben Stahl and Jerry Farnsworth, who did a portrait of President Harry Truman, all had studios here. Following in their footsteps, more recently, Towles Court in Sarasota and Bradenton's Village of the Arts have become artistic communities where sculptors, painters and other artists have homes, studios, and galleries and attract visitors from all over the country.

Famous writers moved to the area to work in tranquility and enjoy the sunshine. On Siesta Key, MacKinlay Kantor, who won a Pulitzer Prize for his novel *Andersonville*, and John D. MacDonald, celebrated mystery writer and creator of the Travis Magee series, were neighbors. Walter Farley, the author of the beloved Black Stallion novels, made Venice his home.

The second great building boom also resulted in what became known as the Sarasota School of Architecture. Led by Ralph Twitchell and his younger partner, Paul Rudolph, its innovative designs of large open spaces, movable screens and rooms opening up onto courtyards and terraces, gathered international attention. The Sanderling Beach Club on Siesta Key, designed by Rudolph, is now on the National Register of Historic Buildings. Their influence has extended into

the present with the works of post-modern architects whose residential and business building designs can be seen all over Sarasota.

The post-war expansion also brought music to the Gulf Coast. In 1948, a local society woman, Mrs. Thomas Butler, spearheaded the drive to start an orchestra in the Sarasota-Bradenton area. A group of local volunteer musicians under the baton of a music director from Tampa gave their first concert in March of 1949. The area took the orchestra to their heart with critical and financial support. In 1955, the Florida West Coast Symphony became the first community orchestra in the United States to own its own rehearsal hall. As the oldest continuing orchestra in the State of Florida, it now has a core of 40 salaried musicians and performs a full classical repertoire from Baroque to Bartok.

The 1960s saw the creation of the Asolo Theater Company by a group of FSU and Yale School of Drama graduates. Started as a theater festival that offered 17th and 18th century comedies during the summer, it became a year-round professional company by 1967, performing a wide range of classical and contemporary European and American plays. Renamed the Asolo Repertory Theatre in 2006, it is one of the few remaining true repertory companies in the country with both conservatory students and a company of professional actors presenting an annual season of plays.

Since then, theater in Sarasota and environs has mushroomed. In 1970, the Van Wezel Performing Arts Hall opened with a stirring performance of "Fiddler on the Roof." The unique building with its eggshell roof designed by the Frank Lloyd Wright Foundation, and lavender and purple color scheme chosen by Wright's widow Oliranna, raised quite a few eyebrows at first. In time, local residents have come to appreciate it, however, and it has become an internationally recognized Sarasota landmark. The Van Wezel's eclectic program features more than 120 performances each year, including Broadway musicals, symphony orchestras, and top national and international music stars, comedians, and dance companies. It provides the other great anchor for the downtown theater district.

That district now includes the Golden Apple Dinner Theatre, which opened its doors in 1971 on Pineapple, down the street from the Edwards Theatre. Since then, it

The newly restored Historic Asolo Theater in the Visitors Pavilion at The John and Mable Ringling Museum of Art.

Rafael Dávila as Canio in *Pagliacci* performed by Sarasota Opera.

has performed more than 270 musicals and plays, including five world premieres. The company has also produced plays for other theaters throughout the U.S. and Canada, Indonesia, China, Malaysia and South Korea.

Two years later saw the beginnings of Florida Studio Theater (FST) as an alternative professional theater company, which toured to area nursing homes, community centers, migrant camps and prisons. In 1977, it moved into its permanent home on North Palm Avenue, occupying the historic Women's Club building. From humble beginnings in a 72-seat theater, it has grown into a multi-million dollar theater complex with 20,000 subscribers a year, offering world premieres and contemporary plays and musicals that have been performed on or off-Broadway in New York. In addition to its mainstage, FST operates a cabaret theater and a smaller stage on First Street. It also has an extensive touring program to Florida schools, teaching children how to write plays. The program culminates in an annual New Playwrights Festival, which receives entries from students all over the world.

In 1979, the Asolo Opera Guild, which had been performing in the old Asolo Theater, purchased the historic Edwards Theater for its new home. At the time,

it was only the seventh opera company in the U.S. to own its own theater. After a full restoration, most of whose funds were raised from individual contributions, the company reopened as the Sarasota Opera in 1984. It offers an annual spring season of four fully staged operas. In 1989, the company began its "Verdi Cycle," dedicating itself to perform all the works of Giuseppe Verdi, including all alternative versions of his operas.

The 1980s saw the formation of the Jazz Club of Sarasota to promote, preserve and educate people about jazz. The club puts on lively concerts throughout the year in area parks, libraries, community centers and concert halls, culminating in the Sarasota Jazz Festival in the spring. One of the largest jazz festivals in the United States, it has featured such star performers as Chick Corea, Eartha Kitt, Dick Hyman and the Count Basie Orchestra.

On the other end of the musical spectrum, the Key Chorale, founded in 1985, debuted with a performance of Handel's rarely heard oratorio "Israel in Egypt." With a core of professional singers, the 130-voice ensemble is dedicated to bringing to life some of the great choral masterpieces, which are beyond the performance capabilities of amateur choral groups.

The Sarasota Ballet of Florida traces its origins back to 1987 as a presenting organization. As a result of enthusiastic community support, it soon became a resident company, the only professional ballet company on Florida's west coast, performing in various venues around town, before finding a permanent home at the FSU Center for the Performing Arts. Its repertoire includes classical ballets such as "Swan Lake" and "Giselle," works by internationally recognized choreographers Alvin Ailey and Ben Stevenson, pieces by contemporary Florida artists, and original works that have received critical acclaim.

Performing arts can be found in a variety of venues.

McCurdy's Comedy Theatre on the North Trail was established in 1988 and has had audiences rolling in the aisles with laughter for years. The list of comedians who have performed there reads like a stand-up's "Who's Who," including Jeff Foxworthy, Chris Rock and Larry "The Cable Guy," and comedy legends like Phyllis Diller, Bob Newhart and the Smothers Brothers.

Beyond Sarasota's immediate boundaries, three energetic community theaters put on a variety of shows. To the north in Bradenton and on Anna Maria Island, the Manatee Players and the Island Players, respectively, offer musicals, comedies and drama. And to the South, the Venice Little Theater, with its two stages and eclectic mix of musicals, contemporary and classical fare, has garnered more awards than any other community theater in Florida and the Southeastern United States.

Over the past decade, the artistic scene throughout the area continues to expand and flower. Following in the footsteps of John Ringling, Circus Sarasota opened its tent flaps in 1997, bringing a one-ring circus with international acts and reputation back to the area, known as "the circus capital of the world."

In addition to these art and cultural organizations, Sarasota hosts a number of internationally recognized art festivals each year, including two chamber music festivals for classical music buffs—La Musica and The Sarasota Music Festival in the summer. Festival Diapente in the spring offers an eclectic mix of food, art, and sounds to appeal to all the five senses and to break down the barriers between different art forms.

Furthermore, the annual Sarasota Film Festival now ranks as the 8th largest film celebration in North America. Since 1998, it has attracted such movie luminaries as Ed Norton, Richard Dreyfuss, Chevy Chase, Felicity Huffman and Robert Altman. Screening more than 200 films over a ten-day period, the festival also offers year-round activities, such as free outdoor Moonlight Movies in Sarasota, Bradenton, Lakewood Ranch and Venice, Monday Night movies at the Asolo theater, and Screenwriters' Circle.

Refurbishing an abandoned lumber yard, a group of local theater enthusiasts created The Backlot, a blackbox performance space to provide local playwrights, actors and visual artists to display their work. Operating like a combination off-off Broadway theater and eclectic performance venue, it allows audiences to enjoy local

SARASOTA OPERA

ESTABLISHED 1960 **www.sarasotaopera.org**

Every winter opera lovers descend on sunny Sarasota Florida for the internationally acclaimed Sarasota Opera Winter Opera Festival. Since its creation in 1960, the company has grown from bringing chamber-sized touring companies to the historic Asolo Theater, to presenting world-class performances with full orchestra and chorus, in productions created specifically for Sarasota Opera. Audiences from all fifty of the United States, and from abroad, attest to its national and international reputation.

The Winter Opera Festival in February and March presents four operas alternating in repertory, mixing audience favorites like Puccini's *La bohème* and Verdi's *La traviata*, with rarely performed works. Operas are staged in traditional romantic productions and sung in the original language with simultaneous English translations projected above the stage.

Sarasota Opera presents internationally recognized singers in leading roles. Many have performed or have gone on to sing with the world's major opera companies including the Metropolitan Opera, London's Royal Opera, and Milan's La Scala. The Sarasota Opera Orchestra is formed specifically to play for the Winter Opera Festival and has been critically praised as one of the country's leading opera orchestras.

Sarasota Opera owns and performs in the historic Sarasota Opera House. This intimate venue with less than 1,200 seats, unparalleled acoustics, and excellent sightlines, is the ideal place to experience an operatic performance. The theater was originally opened in 1926 as the A. B. Edwards Theatre, a vaudeville and movie house with Will Rogers, Sally Rand, the Ziegfeld Follies, Tommy Dorsey, and Elvis Presley among the luminaries who've graced its stage. Purchased by Sarasota Opera in the late 1970's, the theater underwent a series of renovations and reopened in 1984. During 2007–08 the building underwent a $20 million renovation which restored the original glory of the 1920's theater, while creating a venue for opera for the 21st century.

talent in everything from plays to musical events to ball-room dancing exhibitions, film screenings, educational workshops and more.

Two recent arrivals, both professional companies, continue to enhance a burgeoning theater scene. The Banyan Theater Company offers an exciting summer season of three classical and contemporary dramas and comedies, while the Westcoast Black Theatre Troupe celebrates the African-American experience with plays and musicals such as *Black Nativity*, *Fences* and *Dreamgirls*.

There is also a burgeoning music scene in restaurants, coffee shops and night clubs, featuring local bands and solo musical artists. Numerous galleries downtown, on St. Armands, at Towles Court and in Bradenton's Village of the Arts feature art works by local, national and internationally recognized painters and sculptors in various mediums.

Indeed, art continues to pervade every aspect of Sarasota. Walk around town, and you'll see numerous sculptures in front of buildings, in courtyards and along the Tamiami Trail. Because of a city zoning code that any building project over $250,000 has to give one half of one percent of its cost to a public art fund or contribute an equivalent value piece of art, it will only grow. There is also the Sarasota Season of Culture, an annual exhibition that lines Bayfront Park along the Tamiami Trail with monumental pieces of sculpture from November through May. The city has acquired a number of them for permanent installations at libraries and other locations around town.

As the Sarasota area grows, so will its extraordinary art scene, enriching and entertaining both visitors and permanent residents in a cornucopia of art programs no other community in this country can equal. Were he alive today, John Ringling would be pleased.

recreation &
entertainment

recreation &
entertainment

IN ADDITION TO BEING KNOWN AS THE ARTS Capital of Florida, Sarasota is truly a tourist's mecca, a paradise playground for leisure activities, relaxation and fun. The county's 35 miles of Gulf of Mexico coastline boast spectacular beaches. At the same time, there are wonderful inland county and state parks, as well as numerous sports facilities, many of them with international reputations.

With the weather mild and sunny for much of the year—the average temperature is a pleasant 82.2 degrees Fahrenheit—it should come as no surprise that many of the activities and fun start outdoors.

SPORTS
High on the list of favorite sports activities is spring training baseball. The tradition started

in 1926 when the then New York Giants decided that the warm climate provided the perfect place for ball players to get ready for the regular season and made Sarasota their home as part of the Florida "Grapefruit League." Over the years, the Boston Red Sox, the Chicago White Sox and the Baltimore Orioles all spent spring seasons in Sarasota. Michael Jordan played here during the year and a half he took off from basketball to make it as a professional baseball player.

There are two ball parks where people can watch their favorite players shag flies, take batting practice and hone their pitching skills. Both venues are outdoor parks with franks and beer concessions and all the amenities we associate with America's favorite pastime.

The Pittsburgh Pirates have played at Bradenton's McKechnie Field for the past 34 years, including such Hall of Famers as Roberto Clemente and Willie Stargel. Built originally in 1923 in a Florida Spanish Mission style with white stucco on the main grandstand, the stadium was completely renovated in 1993. Night games have

never been played throughout the ball park's history, but there are plans in the works to add lights in time for the 2008 spring training.

Ed Smith Stadium in Sarasota has hosted the Cincinnati Reds since 1998. The 7,500 seat stadium is part of a sport complex that includes four and a half practice fields, a clubhouse and offices. In the summer during the regular season, the Sarasota Reds, a Class A Florida State League team, play over 70 home games there.

When John Hamilton Gillespie came to Sarasota in 1886 and laid out the first 9-hole golf course and clubhouse in the city, he introduced the popular Scottish game to Florida and the United States. Today, more than 60 private, semi-private and public courses dot the region from Palmetto in North Manatee County to Venice, Englewood and North Port in the south. With nearly a quarter of Sarasota residents playing golf, the area is a magnet for fans of the fairways.

As one of America's premier planned communites, Lakewood Ranch has been in the forefront of creating outstanding golf courses with international reputations. The Legacy Golf Club, an 18-hole Arnold Palmer signature course, was ranked by readers of "Florida Golf News" as the number one public course in Southwest Florida. Concessions, named after the famous moment in golf history when Jack Nicholas conceded a two-foot put on the last hole of the Ryder's cup, is an elite private residential golf club. Beautifully landscaped among hammocks of live oak trees, it was designed by Jack Nicholas as a signature 18-hole golf course and opened in 2006.

Lakewood Ranch is also home to the Sarasota Polo Club. Its 130 acres of beautifully manicured lawns are located four miles east of I-75 off University Parkway. The facilities include nine polo fields, a clubhouse and an open-air pavilion. Every Sunday afternoon from mid-December through April, there are matches open to the public. Played on an area the size of nine football fields, polo is a fun, physical and popular event, so much so that tailgating slots are sold out by the end of the summer, although general admission is always available. In March, the club hosts the Triple Crown of Polo, which is broadcast on ESPN. Throughout the year, the Polo clubhouse and pavilion are also available for special events such as weddings, banquets, business seminars and anniversary parties.

Baseball in the Greater Sarasota area is well represented by the Sarasota Reds, among other teams.

COLONY BEACH AND TENNIS RESORT

ESTABLISHED 1969 **www.colonybeachresort.com**

In 1969, Dr. Murray "Murf" Klauber retired from his successful orthodontist practice in Buffalo, N.Y., and, looking for a way to move his family to Sarasota, bought The Colony Beach Club on an 18-acre patch of sand on Longboat Key. Long before Longboat Key emerged as an exclusive enclave for travelers from across the globe, Klauber had the vision on how to turn this collection of 110 then-ragtag beach cottages and two concrete tennis courts into a world-renowned resort.

Over the past 39 years, The Colony has been completely transformed. It now has 234 fully equipped, spacious one- and two-bedroom suites, a grand sweep of private Gulf beach, 21 tennis courts, health spas for men and women, a state-of-the-art fitness center, a highly regarded year-round children's program, designer boutique, pro shop, conference and meeting facilities and one of the finest gourmet waterfront restaurants in the country. The Colony shops, restaurants and spa not only serve as amenities comprising an unparalleled guest experience, but also as destinations sought out by locals and non-resort guests alike. The casually chic environment, superior service, and stunning beachfront location have played a significant part in drawing people to this landmark for over five decades.

To accomplish this tremendous growth, Klauber has drawn on the resource that is most important to him: his family. Today he shares responsibility for the operation of The Colony with his daughter, Katie Klauber Moulton, President and General Manager. Together they direct a Colony family of more than 320 staff, dedicated to making every guest's stay complete perfection. In 2001, for her efforts, *HOTELS* magazine, the leading publication for the global hospitality industry, named Katie Independent Hotelier of the World.

Thanks to that special combination of pioneering vision and the hard work of both him and his family, The Colony Beach & Tennis Resort has risen to the No. 1 tennis resort in the nation for eight consecutive years, according to *Tennis* magazine; has been hailed as "Best in the World" by *Gourmet* magazine and has been recognized by *Child* magazine as being in the top five "Best Family Resorts in the US".

Tennis is another popular sport on the Gulf Coast, and the Nick Bollettieri Tennis Academy in Bradenton has been training many of the world's top tennis players since 1978. Its illustrious alumni include Andre Agassi, Jim Courier, Tommy Haas, Monica Seles and Maria

Fans enjoying tennis at its best.

Sharapova. As a full-time boarding school, the academy combines intensive tennis training with academic education, aiming to develop its students both on and off the court. It also offers part-time programs for juniors, college, professional and adult players.

At the same time, the USPTA Sarasota Tennis League holds tournaments throughout the year at various racquet clubs in the area. Players compete in singles, doubles and mixed doubles at all levels according to their ages and rankings. For amateur lovers of the game, there also are numerous courts in area parks, schools and resorts open to the public.

Another popular spectator sport combines the fluid grace of greyhound racing with the excitement of gaming. Founded in 1929, the Sarasota Kennel Club has offered championship greyhound racing since 1944 at its track near the Sarasota-Bradenton International Airport. Patrons can watch the sleek animals dash around the

oval six days a week, Monday through Saturday from November through April. Two clubhouse dining areas and concession stands throughout the facility offer hot dogs, hamburgers, nachos, sodas and beer as patrons bet trifectas and quinielas and watch the sleek animals dash around the track at break-neck speeds. There is also a brand-new card room, One-Eyed Jacks, which opened in 2006.

For fans of spectator sports willing to venture farther afield, Tampa and St. Petersburg to the north have four professional teams all within an hour's driving distance.

Tropicana Field in St. Petersburg has been home to the Tampa Bay Devil Rays Major League baseball team since 1998. The stadium, which seats 45,000, features one of the world's largest cable supported domed roofs.

Across the bay, the Tampa Bay Buccaneers, winners of the NFL Super Bowl XXXVII in 2003, play at Raymond James Stadium. The facility, with a life-size pirate ship at one end of the field, also hosts concerts, special events and the New Year's Day Outback Bowl. Named the NFL's best stadium in a number of surveys, including the NFL Players Association, it will host Super Bowl XLII in 2009.

The St. Pete Times Forum, which is located in downtown Tampa, is home to two professional teams—the Tampa Bay Lighting ice hockey team, which brought the NHL's Stanley Cup to Florida in 2004, and the Tampa Bay Storm arena football team. When the Storm won ArenaBowl XVII in 2003, it made Tampa the only city ever to win the NFL and Arena Football League championships in the same year.

Tourists and residents who want to partake in athletics can avail themselves of numerous clubs and organizations. Sarasota, Bradenton and Venice all have strong YMCAs, which offer a variety of fitness and athletic programs for children, adults and families. The Sarasota County YMCA, for example, offers exercise classes for adults from low-impact yoga and tai chi to intense cardio spinning and water aerobics. The myriad options for children include adventure camps, climbing and kayaking clubs, ballet, gymnastics, synchronized swimming and flag football.

In addition, there are many other health and fitness centers, such as Gold's Gym, Lifestyle Family Fitness and Curves, which provide easy access to working out throughout the two counties.

SARASOTA POLO CLUB

ESTABLISHED 1991 **www.sarasotapolo.com**

For those who love polo, Florida's best seasons are Spring, Fall and Polo Season! Since 1991, the Sarasota Polo Club has been providing exhilarating polo matches at one of the most beautiful settings in Sarasota. Every Sunday afternoon during polo season, the public is invited to bring out their picnic baskets and enjoy the thrill of the "fastest game on four feet". Spectators partake in the ultimate tailgating experience while 1000 pound polo ponies gallop at full speed just yards away.

The casual ambiance of the Sarasota Polo Club, with its tailgating tradition, appeals to everyone from young couples and families to corporations. With pony and Clydesdale wagon rides, exciting action, half-time entertainment, divot stomping, picnic lunches and

plenty of fresh air, Sunday polo is the perfect place for a family outing; dogs are even welcome on a leash. Businesses welcome the opportunity to entertain clients in a relaxed sporting environment conducive to networking.

Situated on 130 acres, the Sarasota Polo Club boasts nine world-class polo fields, two stick and ball fields and a regulation size arena. Facilities include a member's clubhouse, covered open-air pavilion, three 24-stall barns with turn out, 3/4 mile exercise track, veterinary clinic and gift shop. Surrounding the polo fields are 35 private ranches, ranging from 5 to 40 acres. During season, approximately 600 horses are stabled in and around the Club.

As one of the largest polo clubs in the country, the Sarasota Polo Club hosts many prestigious United States Polo Association (U.S.P.A.) competitions. Polo players from around the globe convene in Sarasota to participate in the multitude of events. The arena school program offers polo instruction to all levels from beginner to expert. The novice player may opt for the comfort of the arena, while introductory lessons are also offered for outdoor grass play.

As one of the most diverse facilities in the area, the Sarasota Polo Club is the perfect location to host any event from corporate seminars and elegant weddings to rustic outdoor festivities. Imagine beautiful sunsets into a wooded landscape as the backdrop for your special occasion.

Located in the award-winning master-planned community of Lakewood Ranch, the Sarasota Polo Club is a truly unique and fascinating destination. Experience Sarasota Polo—the best kept secret on the West Coast of Florida.

LONGBOAT KEY CLUB
AND RESORT

ESTABLISHED 1968 (CLUB) 1982 (RESORT) **www.longboatkeyclub.com**

Play Time

Membership at Longboat Key Club and Resort is a privilege you've earned and one that you'll take pleasure in for years to come. Here, you are among friends, enjoying a wealth of sports, leisure and dining options at the center of the island's most vibrant social scene. Longboat Key Club is more than a place you belong... it's your Island Playground.

Golf

Islandside and Harbourside golf courses offer 45-holes of championship play.

Whether choosing the water challenge of Islandside, or the foliage-filled face-off of newly renovated Harbourside nines, golf experiences are enhanced by views of the Gulf of Mexico or Sarasota Bay.

Tennis

U.S.T.P.A. resident pros offer private lessons, and daily strokes and strategies clinics. All 38 courts are Har-Tru surfaced with several available for evening play. Fully-stocked pro shops offer designer tennis clothing and equipment.

Pool and Beach

Relax and rejuvenate on the immaculate sands of your private beach and pool deck overlooking the Gulf of Mexico. Complimentary beach cabanas, umbrellas and towels are provided, along with beachside food and beverage services.

Island House Spa

The beautiful 9,000 square foot Island House Spa is an oasis of pleasure designed with indulgence in mind. The spa offers 12 treatment rooms with a choice of over 50 services and a large retail boutique.

Fitness

Getting in or staying in shape has never been easier. Choose from personal training sessions at the fully-equipped Fitness Centre or a yoga, spin or step class at the newly opened Mind & Motion Studio.

Member Events

More than 20 events are planned monthly exclusively for Longboat Key Club members: Winemaker dinners, trivia nights, Wine Club, beach bonfires, book clubs, sport championships, and more. News and events are communicated in the monthly magazine, *Club Reflections*.

Newcomers and residents alike are encouraged to visit this exclusive club to learn more about membership opportunities. It's time to play!

For youths and adults, there are organized sports leagues in soccer, football, baseball, softball, volleyball, rowing and basketball at various parks and facilities throughout the county. There is even a senior softball league for players age 60 and beyond.

An adult rugby league plays on the Sarasota Polo grounds. The Sarasota Archery Club is an indoor and outdoor course on 10 wooded acres on 17th Street.

To the north across the Manatee River, the Ellenton Ice & Sports Complex offers ice hockey league and recreational play to children, teens and adult men and women. The figure skating program has produced national contenders. In 2007, Tracy Tanovich and Michael Chau were gold medalists in the State Farm U.S. Figure Skating Championships.

Since 1961, the Sarasota YMCA Sharks swim team has trained young and adult swimmers, attaining an international reputation of excellence. Members have won numerous national YMCA competitions and championships. The Sharks have sent both men and women competitors to the Olympic Games. During the 1996 Olympics in Atlanta, Tripp Schwenk won a silver medal in the 200-meter backstroke and a gold medal as part of the winning U.S. medley-relay team. In 2006, the Sharks added a Masters Swim team to its roster, which has more than 100 swimmers ages 19 to 80, ranging from novice swimmers to national and world champions.

The Sarasota Sharks Triathlon Club, organized under the Sarasota County YMCA to promote triathlon training and racing, welcomes anyone interested in the sport. There are workshops, training sessions and races of various distances. In October, more than 300 athletes participate in the Siesta Key Triathlon. They swim 1000 meters in the Gulf of Mexico, bicycle for 13 miles through the island, and finish with a 3.1-mile run on the beach. Contestants include athletes ages 14 and under to 75 and older, and there are special weight classes, as well as male, female and mixed relay teams.

Games on the beach offer endless opportunities for fun and fitness.

MICHAEL'S ON EAST

ESTABLISHED 1987 **www.bestfood.com**

Celebrates 20 Years of Inspired Cuisine in Sarasota

Entering into the 20th year of service, Michael's On East remains a leader in the fine dining industry undoubtedably due to the restaurant's commitment to exquisite cuisine and extraordinary service. Co-proprietor Michael Klauber's philosophy has always been very simple: to treat his guests the way he would want to be treated. His emphasis on quality permeates every aspect of the restaurant's operation and is displayed in the eclectic menu, artful presentation of the entrées, impeccable service, and intimate ambiance of the restaurant. No detail is too small to come under his watchful eye. And, indeed, it is his own presence, stopping by each of the tables every day, which underscores his commitment to his guests.

The restaurant wasn't the last stop on this epicurean adventure, however. Soon after Michael's On East began to grow, Philip Mancini came on board, giving Sarasota yet another success – Michael's On East Catering. "Philip truly is a phenomenon," said Michael. "He can handle everything from an intimate candlelight dinner for two to a black-tie dinner for 1,000. There isn't very much that he can't do."

Together, Klauber and Mancini have been showered with recognition and awards from "Top Ten Caterers in the U.S.", to the AAA Four-Diamond Award for 14 consecutive years, to Sarasota's Best Place to Be Seen. The haute cuisine, incomparable service and intimate aura create an unparalleled dining experience that has kept it a hotspot in Sarasota for decades.

Klauber explains that he and Mancini "are in the business of creating memorable experiences for our guests, and we look forward to doing so for another 20 years, at least."

Founded on April 27th 1987, Michael's is a collection of fine food and wine establishments including: Michael's On East – fine dining restaurant featuring extraordinary atmosphere, inspired cuisine and intimate piano bar; Michael's On East Catering—creating memorable events from candlelit dinners for two or dazzling galas for 1,000; and Michael's Wine Cellar—wine boutique featuring fine wines, Open House wine tastings, intimate wine dinners and the ability to deliver the world's finest wines to your door through their website.

Water sports and competitions are popular on many of the area's beaches.

With its flat terrain, the Gulf Coast is a great place for bicycle enthusiasts of all ages. Since 1974, the Sarasota-Manatee Bicycle Club has sponsored rides and special events on weekdays, weekday evenings and weekends through scenic areas in both counties. The annual Gulf Coast Cycle Fest in November attracts over 500 cyclists for 15, 30, 60 and 100-mile rides.

In July of 2007, construction got underway on the Legacy Trail, a 12.4-mile path from Sarasota to Venice utilizing the old rail road tracks that linked the two cities. The rail-to-trail project will create a paved corridor up to 12 feet wide to accommodate both bicyclists and runners.

In addition, county and state parks offer many opportunities for biking, hiking and picnicking. Many of these parks are also great places for bird watching. Florida happens to be blessed with the richest diversity of birds in the United States, and about half of the more than 480 species can be found on the Gulf Coast. The keys all are excellent locales for tracking wading and shore birds. The Venice Rookery, a small island in the middle of a lake, and Myakka State Park are wonderful places to see

black-crowned night herons and great egrets. The celery fields east of I-75 near Fruitville Road, which were originally dug out as a flood-control project, have become a wonderful birding habitat, where one can observe bald eagles, wild turkeys, humming birds and snow geese year around.

BEACHES, BOATING AND RESORTS

With a stunningly beautiful bay and world famous white sand beaches, Sarasota County is a paradise for boating, swimming and other maritime activities. From Anna Maria Island in Bradenton in the north to Manasota Key across from Englewood in the south, every one of the barrier islands has public and private beaches. The largest are on Lido Key and Siesta Key fronting Sarasota Bay.

Crescent Beach on Siesta Key with its pristine white sands is world famous. It appears on travel brochures in Europe and Australia. On any day, people come to enjoy the sunshine, swim in the warm waters of the Gulf of Mexico, watch pelicans dive for fish, play beach volleyball and enjoy the spectacular sunset. On

Sunday evenings, an hour before sunset, the community drum circle gathers south of the pavilion. Just follow your ears and you'll find musicians playing maracas, bongos and conga drums, beating out intoxicating rhythms and encouraging wild and wonderful dancing.

Water sports from wind surfing to kayaking, canoeing, diving, snorkeling and fishing in scenic inlets are popular. In 2004, the number of registered recreational boats in Sarasota County hit a record at 6.7 boats per 100 people, higher than the state rate. There are yacht clubs on all the keys and along the coast.

Boat rentals are available at various harbor sites in both Sarasota and Manatee Counties. Marina Jack across the street from downtown Sarasota is host to the county's largest charter boat fleet, including fishing, diving, sailing, cruising and boat rentals. On the northern part of Longboat Key, Cannons Marina has served Sarasota and Manatee Counties for over 50 years. Ranked the top 36th boat dealer in North America by *Boat Industry Magazine* in 2006, it is also one of the few places in Florida recognized by the EPA as a "Clean Marina" and "Clean Boatyard" for its environmentally friendly services.

Each year for four days in June, the Suncoast Offshore Super Boat Grand Prix holds power boat races in Sarasota. The event includes a boat parade, a car show and a motorcycle show and celebration ride. But the main events are the two races in front of Lido Beach when power boats skip across the Gulf waters at breakneck speeds.

The Sarasota Yacht Club's Invitational Regatta, part of the Sarasota Bay Yachting Association Boat of the Year series, became an annual event in 2001 and has brought a renewed focus on sailing to the area.

Another favorite boat event is the annual Holiday Boat Parade in December. Local yachts and sail boats, decked in colorful lights and Christmas decorations parade through the harbor while crowds of people assemble in Bayfront Park to welcome them with hearty "Ho-ho-ho's."

World-class beach resorts on Sarasota Bay and its barrier islands offer visitors everything from luxurious retreats to family vacations to romantic getaways.

Built in classic Mediterranean revival style, The Ritz-Carlton in downtown Sarasota overlooks the bay and blends sophisticated, cosmopolitan elegance with a casual Gulf Coast lifestyle. This AAA Five-Diamond resort offers award-winning dining, an exclusive spa and

Sarasaota offers an exciting nightlife scene.

access to a private beach club, as well as a members-only 18-hole championship golf course, which was named by *Robb Report* as one of the world's best new golf courses for 2006.

Lido Beach, Longboat Key and Siesta Key all have a number of superb waterfront resorts that provide a variety of amenities, including private hot tubs, secluded patios, spas, pools, tennis courts and spectacular views of the Gulf of Mexico.

Among them, the Turtle Beach Resort on Siesta Key with its Caribbean-style cottages was highlighted in the November 2006 issue of *Travel and Leisure Magazine.*

Providing deluxe guest rooms and suites with full kitchen facilities, as well as 6,000 square feet of flexible meeting space, the Lido Beach Resort is a popular place for family vacations and corporate events.

The Colony Beach & Tennis Resort on Longboat Key has been serving people for over 35 years. Considered

one of the world's greatest tennis resorts, it has garnered numerous awards, including *Tennis* magazine's Best Family Resort and Best Game Matching. It is also a popular venue for conferences, catered events and private retreats.

RESTAURANTS AND NIGHTLIFE

Twenty-five years ago, Sarasota was so quiet at night, you could have rolled a bowling ball down Main Street and not have hit anyone. Not any more. Since the area has revitalized with galleries, shops, boutiques and restaurants, downtown has become a busy destination for both daytime and after-hours visitors. With the explosive growth, each year brings even more dining and entertainment venues to both Sarasota and Manatee Counties.

There are now more restaurants per capita in Sarasota than in Manhattan in New York City, providing a wide variety of culinary experiences. If you like ethnic food, you can find Greek, Italian, Thai, Chinese, Cuban, Mexican, Peruvian and German dining throughout the two counties. Because of Sarasota's large Amish population, there are several Amish restaurants, which have lines of customers waiting during the season. Seafood, French, traditional American and contemporary fusion cuisine are all within easy driving distance. Old Florida specialties, including conch fritters, grouper sandwiches and Key Lime Pie, can be found throughout the region.

For nighttime entertainment, many area restaurants and coffee bars have musicians in during the evenings and on weekends, playing everything from folk music to jazz.

The Ritz Carlton's bar, Cà d'Zan, is a popular place to have drinks and enjoy live music and dancing in elegant surroundings.

In downtown Sarasota, the Gator Club features live bands and dancing seven nights a week. Upstairs in the cocktail lounge, a quieter atmosphere prevails. Built in 1913, the Gator Club has been beautifully restored to an Old World, Old Florida décor with antique chandeliers and 100-year-old wood paneling, although the old-fashioned wooden blinds are more recent, left over from when scenes for the movie "Palmetto" were shot there.

There is also the Five O'Clock Club, a neighborhood blues bar on Hillview Street near Sarasota Memorial Hospital, which has live music seven nights a week, showcasing both local and national acts.

On the keys, there are opportunities for dance and music venues on St. Armands Circle and in Siesta Village, where low-key bars and pubs serve tropical drinks under thatch roofed patios. And in Venice, Sharky's On The Pier is a place well worth visiting to listen to bands play while sipping a Bait Bucket Margarita (tequila, lime juice and blue Curacao) and watching the magnificent sunset.

shopping &
area treasures

shopping &
area treasures

WHETHER YOU'RE A SEASONAL RESIDENT, TOURIST or year-around resident, there is always plenty to do on the Gulf Coast. You can go sight-seeing, enjoy the day shopping or set off exploring. The area is rich with historical and cultural attractions, and there are numerous parks and outdoor venues that show off Florida's natural beauty.

SHOPPING

There is an abundance of opportunity for casual and serious shoppers in the Sarasota area. Imagine Fifth Avenue or Rodeo Drive, except surrounded by palm trees and Mediterranean style homes. From contemporary, sophisticated to small village style venues, the area abounds with retail venues. There are quaint neighborhood plazas like Southside Village, emerging shopping

Sarasota boasts extensive shopping opportunities.

neighborhoods like the trendy Rosemary District just north of downtown Sarasota, and large upscale shopping malls. The sheer variety and extent of retail opportunities make the area the leading shopping destination of tourists from all over the world.

Since 2005, when there were more than 2 million square feet of new retail space under construction or announced, the area has continued to grow and prosper. Most visible has been the revitalization of downtown Sarasota, where Main Street has undergone a remarkable renaissance from Selby Five Points Park all the way to U.S. 301. Led by the arrival of Whole Foods as an anchor store, the area has seen the budding of new restaurants; galleries and upscale retail establishments among new luxury high-rise condos. With attractive landscaping and brick sidewalks, Main Street now combines the attractive small town flavor of Florida with 21st century consumer needs.

Closer to the bay, lower Main Street and Palm Avenue offer notable art galleries, designer boutiques, jewelers and spas, intermingled with delightful restaurants, cafes and bistros. Whether you window shop at lunchtime or go on the popular Friday night gallery walks, something wonderful is sure to catch your eye.

Stray a bit farther east and you'll come across Burns Court, just off Pineapple Avenue. This historic part of downtown is home to an art house cinema and a vibrant mix of restaurants, antique shops, gift shops and consignment stores.

Nearby on the eastern edge of downtown, where John Gillespie built his first golf course, lies the Towles Court Art District, a colorful collection of restored 1920s cottages and bungalows set in the midst of tropical gardens and moss-covered oak trees. In this vital colony of more than 40 artist's studios, galleries, cafés and restaurants, you're sure to find art for your home and garden, and art to wear and collect.

To the south on U.S. 41, there are two large shopping malls, both owned by Westfield Group, a multinational company that owns over 120 shopping centers all over the world. Westfield Southgate is Sarasota's most elegant mall, with internationally recognized department stores, including Saks Fifth Avenue, Macy's and Dillards. Sun lit domed ceilings, freestanding retail kiosk and a food court create an appealing atmosphere. Ten miles further south, Westfield Sarasota Square is a more traditional American shopping mall with a wide variety of department stores, specialty shops, an indoor playground, a food court and a brand-new AMC Cineplex. A favorite for mall walkers when the weather gets too hot or rainy outside, this is the place where teens like to hang out, and families shop or take in a movie.

The barrier islands also provide fun-filled shopping opportunities. St. Armands Circle, connected to downtown Sarasota by the Ringling Causeway, is an island emporium with a European flavor, whose clientele includes visitors from all over the world. More than 130 stores, from fancy jewelers and upscale clothing merchants to shops selling beach and tennis apparel, provide something for everyone. Sidewalk cafés and restaurants and a homemade ice cream and fudge eatery cater to jet setters and vacationing families alike.

Siesta Key Village along Ocean Boulevard on Siesta Key is a small neighborhood chock-full of funky bars, gift shops, bistros and ice cream parlors. A great place for browsing when looking for souvenirs, trendy beach attire or fancy evening clothes and jewelry, the area combines an old fishing village charm with a youthful, hip atmosphere.

Downtown Venice on Venice Island has a beautiful wide shopping avenue lined with trees, bushes and flowers. With classic Mediterranean style buildings on either side, you'll find unique galleries and souvenir shops. An historic hotel, quaint tea and coffee houses along with second hand boutiques add to the Old Florida charm and encourage visitors to take a leisurely stroll and window shop.

On the shores of picturesque Lemon Bay in South Sarasota County lies Historic Dearborn Street in the heart of Olde Englewood Village. Recently revitalized, the area offers fine art, hand-crafted gifts, furniture and antiques, casual clothing, vintage furnishings and dining in a relaxed environment. There are also several historic sites and buildings within easy walking distance.

East of I-75 is Lakewood Ranch, the fashionable master-planned community, which attracts visitors from all over the region to its shopping destinations. From Town Center, Market Square and the Lake Osprey Village retail center

to Gateway North, there are restaurants, gift and specialty shops, as well as a wide variety of high-end stores. Main Street, featuring upscale shopping along a tree-lined promenade, has something to thrill even the most sophisticated buyers. The soon-to-be completed San Marco Plaza, architecturally modeled on St. Mark's Square in Venice, Italy, will feature a central piazza with a clock tower, a large fountain and an observation deck. With 65,000 square feet of retail, office and restaurant space, as well as a 250-seat dinner theater, the plaza will make it a true cultural center.

Further up the highway, Prime Outlets in Ellenton is well worth a day trip. Located just 15 miles north of Sarasota on I-75, its village-like tile roofs and friendly pink buildings are visible from the highway. Rated as one of the top 25 outlet shopping centers in the United States by *Value Retail News* in 2007, it boasts more than 135 outlet stores representing many of the world's finest brands at substantial savings.

St. Armand's Circle is just one of Sarasota's shopping locales.

MOTE MARINE LABORATORY

ESTABLISHED 1955 **www.mote.org**

Sarasota's Window to the Sea

Mote Marine Laboratory's origins date back to 1955 when Dr. Eugenie Clark was wooed to the quiet, sparsely populated Charlotte County, FL, by William H. Vanderbilt and his wife Anne, who wanted to start a marine laboratory to satisfy their curiosity about the creatures that lived in the sea. The Lab, first known as the Cape Haze Marine Laboratory, began in a small wooden building, with a dock and a shark pen. Dr. Clark, who would later become known as a foremost shark expert nicknamed "the Shark Lady," was the Lab's first director.

The Lab moved to Siesta Key, and more profound changes occurred between 1965-1966. That's when a unique man stepped forward: William R. Mote was a Tampa native and a successful transportation executive who wanted to use his retirement and energies to do something worthwhile that connected to the sea he loved so much. When he learned of the Lab, he turned his drive and vision to making Cape Haze Marine Laboratory a thriving facility.

Bill Mote recruited Dr. Perry Gilbert, renowned Professor of Zoology at Cornell University, to transform the Lab from a field station to a major research center. A committee of distinguished scientists helped map the Lab's future and, in 1967, the name changed to Mote Marine Laboratory in honor of its major benefactor; significant studies followed.

By 1975, it was clear that Mote Marine Laboratory would need to move from its Siesta Key location. Community leaders rallied. Sarasota City Manager Ken Thompson worked closely with then-State Representative Bob Johnson, Bill Mote and Perry Gilbert to help the Lab move to City Island in 1977. Work later started on a marine science education center, now known as Mote Aquarium, which opened in 1980.

Dr. William Taft, named President in 1978, led the Lab in an era of unprecedented work with a new emphasis on environmental assessment projects, many focusing on Sarasota issues. Dr. Kumar Mahadevan, who today is the Lab's President, joined Mote in 1978 to lead those projects.

Through Mote's leadership, Sarasota Bay was designated into

the National Estuary Program in 1988, Tampa Bay in 1990 and Charlotte Harbor in 1995. The Lab's Center for Shark Research was designated as a National Research Center by the U.S. Congress in 1991. Marine Mammal research also flourished and the Ann and Alfred Goldstein Marine Mammal Center opened in 1994.

Today, Mote's Sarasota Dolphin Research Program is the longest-running study of wild dolphins in history. More recently, Mote has taken a leading role in aquaculture

Florida to operate a joint center in Marine Science to focus increased resources on coastal observation systems, with a special emphasis on biosensors and red tide.

As Mote's research endeavors expanded, so did its educational outreach through popular Aquarium and summer camp programs. Onsite, Mote educators reach more than 50,000 youth per year. Offsite they reach thousands more through SeaTrek videoconferences broadcast from Mote's Keating Marine Education Center.

Today, more than 240 staff members and 1,400 volunteers participate in more than 250 research, education and conservation projects around the world and at home in Southwest Florida. Mote Aquarium draws 400,000 visitors annually, making it the largest attraction in Southwest Florida. With its focus on scientific research, quality educational programming and the public Aquarium, Mote is one of the largest economic development engines in Sarasota County.

Through all of Mote Marine Laboratory's expansion and changes, there is a tremendous sense of spirit shown by the men and women of the Lab. Mote's President and CEO, Dr. Kumar Mahadevan, expresses the feeling best in saying: "It has been 21 years since I took the helm of Mote Marine Laboratory. My excitement for the sea—our last frontier—has not waned. I just hope that Mote will always exist as a place where those in Sarasota and beyond can learn about the sea."

research at Mote Aquaculture Park in eastern Sarasota County. The park is now the largest recirculation aquaculture facility in the U.S. It is designed to further aquaculture as a viable business model for Florida farmers. Mote also developed other field sites in the Florida Keys—on Summerland Key and in Key West—and in Charlotte Harbor. Work in the Florida Keys focuses on coral issues and Charlotte Harbor focuses on fisheries habitat issues, especially concerning Florida's premier game fish, the snook.

In 2006, Mote also signed an historic partnership agreement with the University of South

AREA TREASURES

Although beaches and the arts are the area's best known attractions, Sarasota and its environs have many other attractions, both natural and man-made, that are well worth a visit. Many of them are outdoor venues that take advantage of the tropical climate, which allows plants and flowers to flourish. Others have historical significance, while still others are world-renowned for their special exhibits and collections.

A global leader in marine science, Mote Marine Laboratory is located on a 10.5 acre campus on City Island in the Sarasota Bay. Founded in 1955 by the now-famous shark researcher, Dr. Eugenie Clark, it has evolved from its humble beginnings in a tiny shed into a world-class facility with seven research centers and a staff of 230, including about 40 Ph.D. scientists. Besides exploring coral reefs, coastal ecology, aquaculture marine mammals and fisheries enhancement, the Lab has an education wing, which offers on-site programs for public schools, families and professional and social organizations, as well as a center for volunteers and interns. The Mote Aquarium allows visitors to get up close to sharks, dolphins, manatees and sea turtles and hands on with stingrays, horseshoe crabs and sea stars.

The South Florida Museum in Bradenton is the largest natural and cultural history museum on Florida's Gulf Coast. With over 15,000 artifacts, exhibitions cover a wide range of Florida and local history, from the ice age to the area's aboriginal settlers to the Spanish explorers in the early 1500s. The Bishop Planetarium entertains visitors with digitally programmed astronomy presentations and musical shows. Meanwhile, in the Parker Manatee Aquarium, Snooty the Manatee, one of the area's most beloved sea creatures, provides diversions for families and children. His birthday celebration during an annual Wildlife Awareness Festival is a favorite local event, which includes a birthday card contest and treats for children.

Mote Marine Laboratory is a world-class facility for learning about and experiencing sea life.

MARIE SELBY BOTANICAL GARDENS

ESTABLISHED 1975 **www.selby.org**

Experience Nature Where Fun is in Full Bloom.

The Marie Selby Botanical Gardens in Sarasota, Florida, is a not-for-profit institution fostering understanding and appreciation of tropical plants, especially epiphytes (plants that grow on other plants), through programs of research, conservation, education and display. Selby Gardens is perhaps best known for its living collection of more than 6,000 orchids.

The 9.5-acre bayfront property is an open-air and under-glass museum of more than 20,000 colorful plants, many collected in the wild on more than 150 scientific expeditions to tropical rain forests by Selby Gardens research staff. The stunning Tropical Display House with its

lush rain forest atmosphere, displays unusual flora that can be seen all year around.

Throughout the grounds of the historic Selby estate you will find many distinct gardens: towering Bamboo and Banyan Groves, Cactus and Succulent Garden, and Cycad Collection as well as trees filled with orchids, bromeliads, and other epiphytic plants. Also on the grounds is the former Christy Payne Mansion, a unique example of eclectic Southern Colonial architecture. The Mansion, on the National Register of Historic Places, is home to ever-changing botanical art exhibits.

Children will delight in our brilliant dart frog collection, the koi pond, and our gardens abundant with tropical flora and fauna.

Selby Gardens' Center for Tropical Plant Science and Conservation provides head-quarters for The Bromeliad Identification Center, the Orchid Identification Center and the Selby Gardens' Herbarium.

The Orchid Identification Center (OIC), established in 1975, studies wild-collected and conservatory-grown species orchids and serves as a center for their identification. The Center provides plant identifications to institutions and individuals from around the world.

The Bromeliad Identification Center (BIC) was established in 1979 to honor Mulford B. Foster, one of the world's leading bromeliad collectors. The BIC serves as a source of information for scientists, institutions, and societies on horticultural and botanical aspects of the Bromeliaceae.

The Gesneriad Research Foundation's herbarium and spirit collection was also added to the Gardens in 2002.

The Marie Selby Botanical Gardens has, in short, become a respected center for research and education, as well as a famous showplace that delights more than 180,000 visitors each year.

Selby Gardens is a favored locale at which to view local flora (left), while Jungle Gardens offers entertainment for all ages.

Also located in Bradenton is Cortez, the last remaining fishing village on Florida's Suncoast. Once one of the most important suppliers of seafood on the west coast of Florida, it retains its old Florida charm. This 10-block area encompasses bungalows dating to the 1920s, short narrow roads lined with palm trees and live oaks, and commercial fish houses from the 1940s that are still in use. You can visit A.P. Bell Fish Company to buy wholesale grouper, snapper, shrimp, stone crab and pan fish; or eat at Star Fish Company's dockside restaurant, enjoying an order of mullet and conch fritters. The Cortez Commercial Fishing Festival, held every year in February, attracts more than 20,000 visitors in the course of two days.

The Sarasota Classic Car Museum, located on U.S. 41 across from the FSU Ringling Center for the Cultural Arts, features more than 100 automobiles that span the history of the "horseless carriage" from Model T to Edsel, DeLorean, Bentley and Ferrari. Housed in a newly renovated 30,000 square foot facility, the collection features vintage, classic, muscle and exotic cars, including one of only five Cadillac station wagons ever made, as well as John Lennon's Mercedes Roadster and Paul McCartney's Mini Cooper. Other exhibits include an antique camera and photograph display and an early game arcade.

For those interested in actual racing, the Desoto Super Speedway is just the ticket. The South's fastest short track, a 60 feet wide, 3/8 mile high-banked oval, is located 9 miles east of I-75 on State Road 64 in Manatee County and features Saturday night stock car racing from February through November.

Within Sarasota's city limits are two beautiful and popular gardens. Sarasota Jungle Gardens on Bay Shore Road, south of the Ringling Museum is a 10-acre tropical paradise overgrown with tropical plants, palm trees, native red maples and bald cypress and the largest Norfolk Island Pine in Florida. A stroll along the overgrown trails leads to encounters with pink flamingos, egrets, peacocks and other exotic animals. Visitors can also enjoy a playground, a snack bar and a gift shop, or take in the bird and reptile shows that happen several times each day. One of the highlights is a parrot that performs tricks he did over 50 years ago on the Ed Sullivan Show.

Nature lovers will fall in love with Marie Selby Botanical Gardens on S. Palm Avenue. The legacy of a wealthy couple who were longtime Sarasota residents, the nearly 13-acre estate fronting the Sarasota Bay has a banyan grove, towering bamboo, cacti and eight greenhouses with more than 20,000 plants, plus thousands more in the outdoor gardens. Perhaps best known for its living collection of more than 6,000 orchids, the Gardens has more than 20,000 greenhouse plants and is a center for research and education. Beautifully landscaped, the Gardens attract more than 180,000 visitors a year.

Further to the South, Historic Spanish Point in Osprey is an archeological, historical and environmental site on 30 acres jutting into Little Sarasota Bay. Evidence of Florida's prehistoric past can be seen in the form of a burial mound and two shell mounds that are 5,000 years old. The museum also exhibits Florida's pioneer past through the legacy of the Webb family, which settled here in 1867 and planted citrus trees and built a citrus packing house. In 1910, Chicago philanthropist Bertha Palmer built her winter estate and gardens on Spanish Point. All exhibits are open to visitors with nature trails connecting the historic buildings.

Two state parks offer a variety of outdoor activities and plenty of opportunities to enjoy Florida's natural beauty.

Myakka River State Park, one of the oldest and largest state parks, is a great opportunity to see what Florida looked like before the arrival of European explorers and settlers. Covering 37,000 acres 14 miles east of Sarasota on S.R. 72, it was built in the 1930s by the Civil Conservation Corp. The park is named after the Myakka River, designated as a Florida Wild and Scenic River, which runs through 58 miles of fertile wetlands, dry prairies, shady hammocks and pine flatwoods. It's a popular spot for hiking, biking, freshwater fishing, canoeing, kayaking and camping. Visitors can observe wildlife from a boardwalk that extends along the Upper Myakka Lake and take a stroll among the treetops along the canopy walkway. The world's two largest airboats are available for scenic tours of the lake, and safari tram tours traverse the park's backcountry, offering sightings of deer, alligators, osprey and sandhill cranes.

Oscar Scherer State Park on the South Tamiami Trail in Osprey is a favorite of locals. Visitors can take advantage of its lakes to swim, kayak or canoe, and hike its 15 miles of nature trails. Freshwater and saltwater fishing is available along South Creek and on the shores of Lake Osprey. Noted for its population of scrub jays, which are a threatened species found only in Florida, the park is also home to bald eagles, bobcats, river otters and alligators. There are picnic areas,

Myakka River State Park is named after the Myakka River, which runs through 58 miles of wetlands that are ideal for kayaking and camping.

113

pavilions, full-facility campsites for tents or RVs, and a youth/group campground. A nature center displays exhibits and videos about the park's plant and animal life.

Farther to the south in North Port are The Springs, believed to be the "Original Fountain of Youth" sought by the Spanish explorer Ponce de Leon. The warm Mineral Springs, which originate several thousand feet in the earth's crust, pour 9 million gallons of warm mineral water into a two and a half acre lake whose temperature is 87 degrees year around. With more mineral content that any other spring in the U.S., The Springs can provide relief from many ailments including skin conditions, muscular pain, arthritis, rheumatism and stress. More than 100,000 visitors a year travel from all over the world to soak in the soothing waters. Many come from Europe, Canada and Asia where a high value is placed on the healing powers of mineral spas.

Expand the radius a little and you can find many more delightful attractions throughout the region. From the Sponge Docks in Tarpon Springs north of Tampa to the Thomas Edison Laboratory & Museum in Ft. Myers, the Gulf Coast is a treasure trove that will yield its jewels easily to those willing to pursue them.

networks &
social services

networks &
social services

FOR RETIREES AND YEAR-ROUND RESIDENTS, there is much to brag about in Sarasota, from great beaches and climate, to outstanding art and entertainment, superior health services and education opportunities. No wonder that in 2006, *CNN/Money Magazine* chose Sarasota as America's Best Small City and one of the nations top eight "Best Places to Retire." Also in 2006, Sarasota received the coveted All-American City Award by the National Civic League. The area regularly appears on top ten lists of the most livable places in the United States.

In addition to a superb quality of life, there are other good reasons to relocate to the area. Resources, assets and amenities are important criteria for companies and businesses, especially when considering infrastructure, communication and transportation facilities, as well as social services. In addition to strong showings in all these categories, Sarasota County offers excellent support programs and tax incentives. Our labor force is skilled, well-educated and diverse. It is no accident that in 2003, *Forbes* magazine rated Sarasota 44th "Best Place to Live and Do Business" of the largest 150 U.S. metro areas.

GOVERNANCE

As one of 67 counties in the State of Florida, Sarasota has both incorporated and unincorporated areas. The actual county government consists of a five-member Board of County Commissioners who are elected to four-year terms. They set policies, enact laws and ordinances, and establish county-wide property tax rates. A county administrator identifies needs for services, handles day-to-day operations, and implements policy.

With 3,531 employees and an annual budget of over $1 billion, the County provides police and fire protection, mosquito management and public works, including streets, roads, parks and recreation, water/sewer, wastewater, and numerous other services. Education is administered by the separately elected School Board of Sarasota County, whose jurisdiction includes both the incorporated and unincorporated areas of the County.

The City of Sarasota, which is also the county seat, occupies a relatively small area—25.9 square miles of the county's 571.55 square miles. Of the nearly 380,000 inhabitants of the county in 2006, only 55,364 belonged to the city proper, but many living in unincorporated areas refer to themselves as Sarasota residents. The city also has a commission whose five members are elected to four-year terms. The position of mayor rotates among the members each year while a city manager takes care of the day-to-day business.

There are three other self-governing communities within county limits: the cities of Venice and North Port, and the town of Longboat Key. Each has separate commissions or city councils as governing bodies, which are responsible for local police and fire protection, and oversee public works, such as streets, roads, water/sewer and other local city and town services.

The county or each city provides its own police and fire departments. Similarly, separate water/sewer services and garbage/trash collection and recycling programs for residents are available throughout the county and municipal services. The county operates solid waste/landfill facilities. Commercial customers can use a variety of solid waste removal services in

Public art can be found throughout the city of Sarasota.

CITY OF SARASOTA

ESTABLISHED 1902 www.sarasotagov.com

The City of Sarasota, with a population of approximately 55,000, lives up to its slogan daily as a place "where urban amenities meet small town living." Residents, whose median age is 41, are active, involved with their community, and enjoy the diverse amenities the City offers.

Many Sarasota residents enjoy the cafes, shops and art galleries in the downtown. Ten years ago, it was joked that you could roll a bowling ball down Main Street and not hit a single car or pedestrian it was so empty. Today, the downtown is alive with activity, thanks to City leaders' commitment to revitalization. Since 1987, the City has reinvested $44.7 million dollars into downtown infrastructure projects including park improvements, land banking for public parking and streetscape improvements.

In 2001, with the esteemed guidance of world renowned urban planner Andres Duany, City planners, residents and the business community drafted a downtown master plan in part to help attract people back to the downtown. Much of the plan is a tremendous success with developers investing in the area and people subsequently calling downtown home. Since 2002, about 800 residential units have been built, many of which are connected to mixed-use developments, and another 1,200 units are approved to

begin construction. Downtown is now vibrant, livable and quite resident friendly with two thriving grocery stores.

The City of Sarasota is committed to recreation and the cultural arts, owning and operating three popular venues: the Van Wezel Performing Arts Hall, which hosts about 100 performances each year; Bobby Jones Golf Club, one of the most popular public courses in the area; and Ed Smith Stadium,

home of the Cincinnati Reds during spring training and many other community events.

Sarasota embraces its green spaces, with nearly 50 designated public parks, including Fredd "Glossie" Atkins Park, a popular gateway into the City from the north, and Payne Park, which will be Sarasota's answer to Central Park. From parks to cultural arts to athletics, the City of Sarasota offers the amenities of a large city, yet retains its small town appeal.

COMCAST

ESTABLISHED 1966 **www.comcast.com**

Tomorrow's Technology Today

From humble beginnings in the early 1960's, Comcast has grown from a small provider offering a handful of TV channels to a broadband powerhouse that has changed the way customers view television, use the Internet, and make telephone calls. Comcast has over 500 employees locally, which has been an important part of the Comcast legacy since opening its doors in 1966.

What's driving Comcast's growth and evolution? Comcast puts the customer in control. The company is rapidly transitioning its entire industry to the digital age, which means not only hundreds of additional channels, but better quality, more innovative, and newer services and enhancements through Comcast Digital Voice, ON DEMAND, high-speed Internet, high-definition television and digital video recorders.

Comcast is keeping the customer service experience local. No matter how advanced the services become, it is important to Comcast to continue to improve the delivery of products, making the process as easy as possible for customers and treating each individual customer with the care, courtesy and time each customer deserves.

Comcast understands that competition is the most pro-consumer policy there is and the company is thriving in a competitive world today. Although competition tends to add excitement in any industry, competition alone didn't drive the enhancements that Comcast customers have enjoyed over the past five to ten years in West Florida. Comcast built its fiber optic network over ten years ago and continues to enhance its investment. That has always been the Comcast plan to consistently give customers more value for their dollar and to build upon its investments in new technology to bring new products and services to its customers first.

Comcast is also committed to its local communities through Comcast Cares Day, Cable in the Classroom, Comcast Foundation grants, and its association with United Way along with other community sponsorships, projects and special events.

For more information about Comcast, please visit Comcast's website.

the incorporated areas of the county. In the unincorporated areas, businesses must contract with a private waste removal company.

Because local governments in Florida operate "in the sunshine," nearly all council and commission meetings and workshops are open to the public. Both Sarasota City and County board meetings are televised on local cable stations.

UTILITIES

Verizon has been the primary telephone service provider to residents and business customers, offering fiber-optic and digital optic capabilities to all industrial and commercial zones in Sarasota County. But new developments in telecommunications are underway. With the industry's need for speed and access, the area's county voice, data and video services are retooling their distribution systems with next-generation broadband technologies.

Comcast of West Florida, the dominant cable company in the county, has been providing high definition television, video on demand and high-speed Internet access. More recently, it has added Comcast Digital Voice service, offering customers digital-quality phone service with unlimited direct-dial local and long distance calling, including Web access to voice mail.

In 2005, Verizon began to replace the copper wires that connect customer homes and businesses to the Verizon network with "fiber to the premises" (FTTP) fiber-optic technology in the county. The fiber-optic cable represents bandwith and speed for next-generation FIOS Internet access and voice and video applications. As a result, Verizon now offers a competitive alternative to Comcast's bundle of Internet, television and telephone services.

Florida Power & Light Company (FPL) provides electrical power to all but a small portion of Sarasota County's homes, businesses and industry. One of the largest and fastest growing utilities in the United States, it expects to add more than 80,000 customer accounts annually and plans to build new power plants using diverse fuel mix and purchase power to meet increasing demand. For commercial/industrial customers, the utility offers different categories of rate schedules,

Sarasota lights up every evening.

THE GREATER SARASOTA CHAMBER OF COMMERCE

ESTABLISHED 1920 www.sarasotachamber.com

Your Chamber Leading the Way

Sarasota, Florida is consistently identified as one of America's most desirable places to live, work, and raise a family. Clean air, sparkling white sand beaches and a sunny climate have made it world famous as a center for the good life, and the vibrant recreational and cultural scene offers activities for every taste and budget. Greater Sarasota is a diverse community of big city amenities and small town ease of living. Business owners and employees enjoy not only the good life, but a thriving business climate. Top-rated schools, a motivated workforce and high quality of life make Sarasota home to some of the most successful and productive companies in the country.

Relocating to the greater Sarasota area can go smoothly with the help of The Greater Sarasota Chamber of Commerce, a not-for-profit membership organization that exists to maximize its members' success, the community's competitiveness, and the area's economic strength. Individuals and families who want to move to Sarasota can visit www.sarasotachamber.com to find a home, find a great job through links to The Chamber's partner organizations, check out the myriad leisure activities and learn about all those details of daily living they need to know—educational opportunities, registering to vote, getting a license plate, locating health care and more. New or "soon-to-be" residents can also visit The Chamber on-site, where its friendly staff can offer information to ease the relocation process via relocation packets, maps of the area and more.

With a wealth of options and plenty of resources, Sarasota County is also a great place to do business. Companies already in the area say the quality of life, modern infrastructure, tax incentives and qualified workforce all contribute to their success of doing business here.

Leadership is essential to the growth and prosperity of the community, and The Greater Sarasota Chamber of Commerce is emerging as a leading voice of Florida's Suncoast. Responding to the needs of its members, The Chamber strives to keep programs current and responsive to the demands of the area's modern business climate. The Chamber works to maintain a prosperous greater Sarasota – a great balance of lifestyle benefits and a successful, sustainable business community that offers high quality jobs, hence its tagline— "Good Life. Good Business."

For nearly a century, The Chamber has been an agent of change, building bridges between the private sector and local government, residents and other stakeholders. Since incorporation, the organization has expanded into four divisions and seven councils serving The Chamber's constituents—the community, businesses and individuals. The Chamber works each day with its membership and the entire community to create plans and initiatives that will benefit the region as a whole.

There has been amazing work contributed by the various councils of The Chamber. Leadership Sarasota County is a premier annual leadership training program for up-and-comers and fields a class of the community's brightest future leaders. The Young Professionals Group, a meaningful networking organization of dedicated, talented young professionals between ages 21 to 40 in Sarasota County, strives to enrich the community by uniting and developing its young professionals.

The Small Business Council provides business referrals and reliability information, informing potential customers that a member company is deserving of their trust, while also providing the Frank G. Berlin, Sr. Small Business Resource Center, free small business counseling sessions and high-impact seminars geared toward the busy professional through its Chamber University program.

Equally notable is the work accomplished by members of The Chamber's Commerce Sarasota Council (CSC) and

Governmental Issues Council (GIC), the driving forces behind making "good life" and "good business" perfect embodiments of greater Sarasota. The councils work closely with business, government and other community and civic organizations to coordinate economic development initiatives that diversify Sarasota County's economy. The CSC works with the private sector and the community to help existing businesses profit and grow.

The International Business Council provides opportunities for people interested in international business to connect, expands international relationships and

exchanges, and creates more jobs, income, tax revenue and economic benefits for greater Sarasota.

Additionally, the Membership Benefits and Events Council focuses on member benefits— exclusive discounts on goods and services that can help run a more profitable business. Countless networking events, golf tournaments and other special events, in addition to cost-effective marketing vehicles and volunteer positions on committees and task forces all provide unparalleled opportunities for a member.

Over the years, hundreds of businesses and organizations have joined the ranks of nearly 2,400 member companies, representing tens of thousands of employees. Whether it's through new business development and networking opportunities, easy access to economic and market data or taking advantage of a variety of advertising opportunities, Chamber members have learned that their investment in The Greater Sarasota Chamber of Commerce is a valuable asset.

depending on level of demand. Encouraging voluntary customer conservation, it also offers significant cost-saving incentives in the form of load management and conservation programs for businesses and industry.

The Peace River Electric Cooperative (PRECO) serves a portion of the northeastern part of Sarasota County. A not-for-profit distribution cooperative, it provides retail electric service to more than 30,400 families, business and industry in parts of ten Florida counties.

Natural gas can be obtained from People's Gas in most industrial and commercially zoned areas of the county. A subsidiary of TECO Energy, a $9.5 million energy giant headquartered in Tampa, it is one of the largest providers of natural gas statewide, and has served residential, commercial and industrial customers in Sarasota County for 30 years. People's Gas also offers a number of incentive-based energy conservation programs. The opening in 2002 of its Gulfstream Natural Gas System Pipeline, which runs along the bottom of the Gulf of Mexico, from Alabama to just south of Tampa, increased gas flow capacity into Florida by 50 percent.

TAXES

With seven percent sales tax, Florida has one of the lowest rates in the nation. It is also the only state in the Southeast with no personal income tax.

Sarasota County charges a tourist development tax of four percent on rentals of six months or less. Rentals include hotels, motels, apartments, condos, houses, beach houses or cottages and boats that have permanent fixed locations at a dock. Most of the funds are used for beach maintenance, restoration and erosion control. The revenue also underwrites tourist advertisement and promotions and provides grants for cultural and arts activities, including festivals, that bring tourist visitors to Sarasota County.

Sarasota County property owners pay a millage rate of about $16 per thousand dollars of taxable property. Rates vary depending on city, town or unincorporated county area. The revenue funds city and county budgets, the Sarasota County School District, Sarasota Memorial Health Care System, Mosquito Control and Emergency Medical Services.

Florida also provides a $25,000 homestead exemption for homeowners whose property is their primary residence. A homeowner must have title or record as of January 1 and reside permanently on the property in order to qualify for the deduction of $25,000 from the total appraised tax value.

TRANSPORTATION

There are two primary traffic arteries than run through the county from north to south. Paralleling the coastline is U.S. 41, also known as the Tamiami Trail because it was the original connecting road between Tampa and Miami. Four to five miles to the east is Interstate 75 (I-75), which was completed in the mid-1980s. Most long distance, inter-regional and interstate traffic relies on I-75. As development increases to both sides of I-75, an increasing number of east-west highways provides efficient connectors between the two north-south traffic routes. Most east-west traffic within the county occurs in and around the cities of Sarasota and Venice.

Public transportation is available in the urbanized areas of the county in the form of bus service by the Sarasota County Area Transit system (SCAT). Publicly owned and operated, SCAT runs on fixed schedules for about twelve hours a day, six days a week.

For longer distances, the Greyhound Lines, Inc., as well as several charter bus companies connect the area to other parts of Florida and the rest of the United States.

A regional infrastructure of world-class airports and deep-water ports provides both passenger service and freight shipping worldwide. Indeed, Sarasota County is within easy driving distance of four international airports.

The Sarasota Bradenton International Airport (SRQ) serves as a gateway to the Gulf Coast for more than 1.5 million travelers each year. Located at the intersection of U.S. 41 and University Parkway on the Sarasota and Manatee County line, it offers comfortable and convenient facilities and a stress-free atmosphere. With two runways and seven major and two commuter airlines, it provides access to domestic and international destinations through connecting hubs and daily non-stop flights. To meet the increasing demand in the corporate jet market, in 2005, the airport expanded the existing two fixed-base operators (FBOs) and added a third.

To the north, Tampa International Airport (TPA) and St. Petersburg-Clearwater International Airport (OIE) are two major U.S. and international air portals, which provide commercial and general aviation services.

SARASOTA BRADENTON INTERNATIONAL AIRPORT

ESTABLISHED 1939 www.srq-airport.com

Welcome to Sarasota Bradenton International Airport (SRQ), your world-class aviation gateway to Florida's Gulf Coast, with their famous white-sand beaches only minutes away.

Often described as the relaxing side of Florida, the Sarasota-Bradenton area offers a less crowded, more laid-back approach to the Sunshine State. It is conveniently located in the center of a region full of exciting attractions, unique shops and the thriving, culture-rich communities of Sarasota and Bradenton.

A modern, comfortable and secure facility, SRQ International offers all of the amenities you expect; rental car services, a full service food area, duty-free shopping and free Wi-Fi access inside the terminal. International airlines provide scheduled and charter services, making worldwide connections possible. Whether you're flying for pleasure or business, you'll be flying stress-free at competitive prices.

The Sarasota-Bradenton extended catchment area connects to 61% of Florida's population within 150 miles via Interstate 75 and US Highway 41.

Drive time to other major Florida cities:

- St. Petersburg—45 minutes (40 miles / 65 km)
- Tampa—one hour (57 miles / 92 km)
- Ft. Myers—one hour, 30 minutes (90 miles / 145 km)
- Orlando—two hours (129 miles / 209 km)
- Miami—four hours (223 miles / 360 km)

SRQ International's facilities are designed to expedite the travel experience and maximize comfort and convenience. Find more about their conveniently located facility and extensive route network on their website.

HERALD-TRIBUNE MEDIA GROUP

ESTABLISHED 1925 **www.heraldtribune.com**

Like the communities it serves, the *Sarasota Herald-Tribune* has grown and diversified in ways that seemed unimaginable in 1925, when its first editions rolled off the presses.

What began as a small, morning daily has grown into the largest news operation in Southwest Florida. Multiple newsrooms contribute to six zoned editions each day, a 24-hour television channel, a website, a magazine group and other news and advertising ventures.

Anchoring the Herald-Tribune Media Group is its sleek, new headquarters on Sarasota's Main Street just blocks from its original newsroom.

David B. Lindsay and his younger brother, Dick, second-generation newspapermen from Marion, IN, saw an opportunity to launch a newspaper in Sarasota and published the first edition of the *Sarasota Herald* on Oct. 5, 1925, in what is now the Woman's Exchange consignment shop on Orange Avenue in downtown Sarasota.

It became an afternoon publication in 1929. When the Lindsays acquired the competing publication, the *Sarasota Tribune* in 1938, the *Sarasota Herald* became the *Sarasota Herald-Tribune*. The *Herald-Tribune* returned to morning publication in 1952, when the Lindsays introduced a new afternoon daily, the *Sarasota Journal*, which was published until 1982.

Above: The design of the Herald-Tribune Media Group's new, $27 million headquarters in downtown Sarasota pays homage to the Sarasota School of Architecture. Right: In addition to its newspaper and Internet operations, the Herald-Tribune's main office includes an expanded television studio for its 24-hour cable news program.

That was the same year The New York Times Co. purchased the successful, family-owned newspaper from the paper's second publisher, David B. Lindsay Jr.

In 1995, the *Herald-Tribune* was one of the first newspapers in the country to launch a 24-hour television operation. What is now SNN News 6 was created in partnership with Comcast Cablevision.

In 2006, the *Herald-Tribune* vacated the cramped and retrofitted headquarters it had occupied for nearly 50 years on U.S. 41 and moved into its new, $27 million headquarters that blends Sarasota's architectural history with state-of-the-art technology.

In addition to the 850,000 people who live in Sarasota, Manatee, Charlotte and DeSoto counties, the Herald-Tribune Media Group's newspaper and television operations reach a worldwide audience through its award-winning website, heraldtribune.com, introduced in 1997.

The news organization's print, television and Internet operations also provide multiple platforms for advertisers to reach Southwest Florida's residents and visitors.

Technological advancements and the public's changing appetite for how and when it wants the latest headlines and community news will continue to bring about changes at the Herald-Tribune Media Group, but its mission to inform the communities it serves remains unchanged.

To the south, Southwest Florida International Airport (RSW) in Ft. Myers has a capacity for 10 million passengers annually and provides general aviation services to corporate, commercial and private aviators.

In addition, the Venice Municipal Airport (VNC) with two 5,000 feet intersecting runways is an alternate landing site for corporate aircraft and offers air charter, air taxi and flight instruction. There are more than 200 aircraft based at VNC, and about 80 aircraft owners are on a waiting list for hangar space.

Port Manatee, the fifth largest of Florida's 14 deepwater seaports, is located on Tampa Bay, 17 miles north of Sarasota County in northwestern Manatee County. With six deepwater berths and more than 1 million square feet of office and warehouse space, it is Fresh Del Monte Produce's second largest U.S. Port facility and the Southeast's leader for forestry product imports. It is also the closest U.S. deepwater seaport to the Panama Canal, providing shippers with speedy access to South American and Pacific Rim markets.

The Port of Tampa handles nearly 50 million tons of containerized and bulk cargo each year. As the 11th largest port in the U.S., it has the largest dockside cold storage facility in North America. Its scheduled container service provides regular connections to North and South America, Europe and Asia, connecting Southwest Florida with ports all over the world.

Rail transportation in Sarasota County is limited to freight service—the nearest available Amtrak passenger service is in the city of Tampa. The Seminole Gulf Railway, a short-line railroad, operates along a corridor that runs north of the City of Venice through the City of Sarasota. Its two lines connect with CSX Transportation, one of the nation's major companies providing rail, intermodal and rail-to-truck transload services. CSX serves Port Manatee and the Port of Tampa, where it operates a major rail yard with links to commercial markets in 23 eastern states, the District of Columbia and two Canadian provinces. All industrial sites in the county, however, can utilize intermodal freight services.

MEDIA

Just as commercial goods and passenger traffic needs good transportation conduits to flow, so successful communication requires outstanding media channels.

Sarasota County is located near both Port Manatee and the Port of Tampa.

As an area of culture, creativity, and high-tech, Sarasota can count on a variety of local, national and international media outlets.

Television stations serving the region include ABC, NBC, CBS and FOX affiliates, public television and local cable and news channels. The area is home to ten radio stations and receives 40 more stations from neighboring counties. Listeners can find everything from all-news to jazz, sports, classical, rock, Hispanic and country.

The area's flagship daily newspaper is the *Sarasota Herald-Tribune*, which has been owned by the New York Times Company since 1982. With multiple daily zoned editions and an average of 73 pages daily and 159 pages on Sunday, it combines regional and state news with outstanding local coverage. The Herald-Tribune Media Group also has a 24-hour cable television news station, SNN News 6, which reaches more that 180,000 viewers, representing more local news viewers than all other area television stations, including those in Tampa and Ft. Myers.

ECONOMIC DEVELOPMENT CORPORATION
OF SARASOTA COUNTY

ESTABLISHED 2004 www.edcsarasotacounty.com

Prosperity by Design

Sarasota County has a flourishing economy strengthened by diverse and dynamic local businesses. Top-ranking schools, an excellent job market and award-winning healthcare are a few reasons why we have garnered national attention in recent years. Sarasota County's strong economy, enhanced by a fantastic quality of life, has earned us a spot on *Forbes Magazine's* "Best Place to Live and Do Business", and the name "Best Small City in the United States," by *Money Magazine*.

As our coastal paradise shines in the spotlight, the Economic Development Corporation of Sarasota County is helping to shape a diverse, sustainable economy while enhancing the area's unique natural and cultural environment.

Our community's many assets include a skilled labor force, close proximity to air and shipping routes, favorable economic and tax incentives and a quality of life that is second to none.

Those factors allow local businesses to be among the country's most productive. The gross metropolitan product, or economic value produced by Sarasota-Bradenton businesses, continues to increase at a rate faster than most other metro regions. So too has our job growth. In fact, Sarasota was ranked 11th overall and third for job growth on *Forbes Magazine's* 2007 list of "Best Cities for Jobs."

Sarasota County provides a good climate for entrepreneurial development and was recently recognized by *BizJournal* as the second best market to grow a small business. Our community's entrepreneurial spirit, dedicated workforce, globally competitive businesses and cultural assets ensure that the future of Sarasota County remains vibrant. We're carefully creating "Prosperity by Design."

SARASOTA AND HER ISLANDS CONVENTION & VISITORS BUREAU

ESTABLISHED 1986 www.sarasotafl.org

Imagination. Creation. Vacation.

From the imagination of John Ringling to the "Finest, Whitest Sands in the World," Sarasota and Her Islands—situated on Florida's Gulf Coast—offers visitors an atmosphere of cultural indulgence and creative abundance. From the satin-soft sands of Siesta Key to the acoustic acclaims of the Van Wezel Performing Arts Hall in downtown Sarasota, travelers enjoy the relaxing atmosphere of a beach side bungalow just minutes from cosmopolitan and cultural amenities that rival major metropolitan centers.

Recently named again to Dr. Beach's "Top 10 Beaches in America," Sarasota's Siesta Key holds the worthy title for the finest, whitest sand in the world, as judged by the Woods Hole Oceanographic Institution. Each of Sarasota's

islands and beaches touts a distinctive character, from key lime quaint to opulent elegance.

More than just sand, sun and surf, Sarasota and Her Islands stimulates the creative adventurer with a variety of museums, artist galleries, theatres and stand-alone masterpieces. Whether touring the Ringling Museum of Art, the Sarasota Opera House, or the artists' colony at Towles Court, travelers discover a number of exceptional cultural outlets amidst the sands of Sarasota and Her Islands.

From perusing one-of-a-kind specialty shops to thriving in a major mall setting, Sarasota provides everything from premier outlets and upscale shopping to beachfront boutiques. Shop-aholics beware—the allure of

St. Armands Circle is hard to escape with a shop for every whim. For charming downtown shopping, travelers visit Venice to the south, picking up trinkets and treasures, including the areas famous collection of pre-historic sharks teeth. After working up an appetite, travelers satisfy their palate at a variety of independent and unique dining venues, from waterfront dining at Turtles on Little Sarasota Bay to Michael's On East and Derek's Culinary Casual in downtown Sarasota.

With accommodations ranging from beachfront bungalows to upscale resorts and a variety of special events year-round, Sarasota and Her Islands offer travelers an ideal destination for romance, business, family fun and exploration.

THE COMMUNITY FOUNDATION OF SARASOTA COUNTY

ESTABLISHED 1979 www.cfsarasota.org

Connecting Donors who Care with Causes that Matter For Good. For Ever. ®

When it comes to innovative support of health and human services, the arts, the environment, animal welfare, education and more, the Community Foundation of Sarasota County has led the way for over 28 years.

Back in 1979, a group of visionary leaders from the Southwest Florida Estate Planning Council got together to form an organization that would serve as the bridge between their clients who wished to establish permanent charitable funds for the purpose of helping others and non-profit agencies that provide direct services throughout the area. They created the Community Foundation of Sarasota County, a public charity with roots that stretch back to 1914, when the first community foundation began. Today, there are more than 700 locally controlled community foundations across the nation united by a single mission: improving the quality of life in a community through the establishment of permanent charitable funds, well invested, that generate millions of dollars each year in grants and scholarships that support the causes that caring donors care about the most.

Above: The Community Foundation of Sarasota County, located at The Leila & Michael Gompertz Center

Right: Stewart Stearns, President & CEO of the Community Foundation of Sarasota County receives an award from Sarasota County Schools Superintendent Gary Norris for the Performance Based Diploma Program grant from the Jo Bowen Nobbe Fund of the Community Foundation. This grant provides for a new dropout prevention program for at-risk students that currently operates in every high school throughout the county.

From its modest beginnings with just a single volunteer, a telephone and a board of directors that believed in the value of making charitable giving work for the community, the Community Foundation of Sarasota County has grown to more than 580 charitable funds and $150 million in assets, awarding over $6 million in grants and scholarships each year. In addition, the Nonprofit Resource Center supports thousands of charitable organizations in the fulfillment of their missions through workshops, trainings, consulting and staffing resources and peer-to-peer learning experiences.

In the grand scheme, the Community Foundation is a valuable community resource that responds to all kinds of emerging needs...and a personal, flexible and permanent vehicle for philanthropy that is truly here For good. For ever. ®

TIDEWELL HOSPICE AND PALLIATIVE CARE

ESTABLISHED 1980 **www.tidewell.org**

TideWell Hospice and Palliative Care is an independent, not-for-profit organization offering a home-based, total support system for patients and families dealing with advanced illness. TideWell was founded in 1980 in Sarasota and expanded over the intervening years to serve Manatee, Charlotte and DeSoto counties.

Home-based palliative, or comfort care is the basic premise of the program, involving the support of physicians, registered nurses, social service counselors, home health aides, chaplains and volunteers, all following a prescribed plan of care. TideWell's services are available to everyone, regardless of ability to pay.

In choosing TideWell, patients and families make a decision to spend their last months together in a familiar and caring environment. With TideWell's supportive services, there's a sense of relief as trained professionals offer care and guidance. Experts in pain and symptom control, TideWell staff focus on continuity of care, addressing the physical, psychological, social and spiritual needs of patients and families.

The rewards of caring for those who are at the end of life are many and account for the growth of hospice care across the nation. Nowhere is it more evident than on Florida's Gulf Coast, where TideWell will care for approximately 6,000 patients this year.

One of the greatest hopes for dying patients is to be pain-free and to have distressing symptoms controlled. Early on, hospice learned that quality of life revolves around these two factors, and only when they are controlled can people reach beyond to the comforts and therapeutic healing of mind and spirit.

Decisions are made based on the individualized needs of patients, with the realization that something more can always be done to bring comfort and dignity to those dealing with advanced illness.

Although hospice is often perceived as a service just for cancer patients, TideWell admits patients with a broad range of diagnoses including heart and lung disease, AIDS, renal failure, Amyotrophic Lateral Sclerosis (ALS) and end-stage Alzheimer's. Any disease with a predictable prognosis of six months or less is within TideWell's admission criteria.

Rather than a place, hospice is a philosophy — a program of care and support wherever patients need us. TideWell's services extend to any location — a home, the hospital, an assisted living facility (ALF), a nursing home or any of our seven Hospice Houses. No one needs to die alone as TideWell Hospice and Palliative Care reaches out to any setting to provide full support.

Venice, North Port and Englewood also have daily newspapers. In addition, local weekly publications include the *Longboat Observer, Sarasota Observer, Tempo News, Siete Dias, Creative Loafing,* Siesta Key's *Pelican Press* and the *Gulf Coast Business Review,* a business newspaper. Sarasota County also is home to nine magazines whose special interests include business, the arts and the social scene.

SOCIAL SERVICES

In addition to city and county-wide social services, Sarasota's populace supports numerous not-for-profit and charitable organizations, both financially and through extraordinary volunteerism. Organizations like the Selby Foundation, The Community Foundation of Sarasota County and the Gulf Coast Community Foundation are leaders in providing grants for worthy causes. During the winter season, there are so many galas, auctions, fundraisers and other charity events that scheduling them all becomes quite a challenge.

You can find local branches of national organizations, such as United Way, Boys and Girls Clubs Inc., Habitat for Humanity, the American Cancer Society, the Salvation Army and the YMCA, which do superior work in their areas of concern. Goodwill Industries-Manasota, Inc., for example, has outlets throughout Sarasota and Manatee Counties and has been so successful that it has become a model for other Goodwill organizations in the U.S.

At the same time, there is a cornucopia of local social service organizations, such as the Women's Resource Center, Safe Place and Rape Crisis Center of Sarasota (SPARCC), Pet Therapy, Inc., and All Faith's Food Bank, to name a few.

One of the largest local organizations is Florida Wine Fest & Auction, which serves disadvantaged children and youth in the Sarasota area. The annual event, which takes place in April, is one of the largest events of its kind in the U.S., attracting vintners and chefs from around the world. Over the past 17 years, the charity wine auction has raised more than $6.1 million and has supported over 70 different charitable agencies. Operating year-round with a paid staff of only two, the organization operates with a large cadre of volunteers that contribute more than 45,000 man hours each year.

With an abundance and variety of worthy causes, each with their champions and dedicated volunteers, it is no wonder that the Sarasota area is among the highest in the nation for charitable giving.

manufacturing
& technology

manufacturing
& technology

WITH TOURISM, LEISURE AND RETIREMENT SERVICES representing the most visible industries on the Gulf Coast, it may come as a surprise that the Sarasota area is also home to a host of innovative manufacturing companies whose impact reaches far beyond the local community. A growing number of national and international companies call Sarasota home. Largely unnoticed by the community, they design and manufacture products that are used all over the world.

PPi Technologies Global in Sarasota, for example, a packaging company with international reach, produces sealable pouches and trays for thousands of name-brand products in the medical, pharmaceutical and food industries. Chances are you have some of them in your home and kitchen. Since its inception in 1996, it has won numerous awards for its innovative designs and entrepreneurial success.

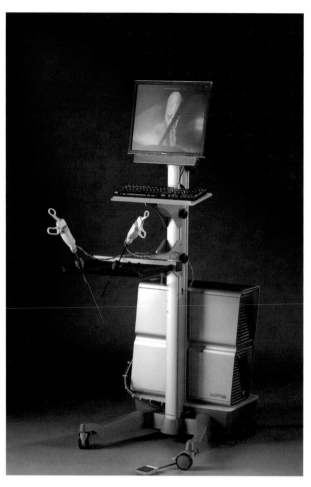

South Sun Energy Conservations Corp., another industry leader that manufactures Winsulator interior storm windows, providing effective energy conservation, was used by NASA at the Kennedy Space Center to remedy an overheating problem that they were experiencing.

One of the area's most unusual success stories is Sun Hydraulics Corp., which has manufactured hydraulic valves and manifolds that control industrial and construction machinery since 1970. Ranked 14th among *Forbes* Small Business 100, it has operations at three U.S. facilities and in France, Germany, the United Kingdom, Korea and China. At the same time, Sun Hydraulics has operated under a unique business model for engineering companies that brings visitors and observers from all over the world. There are no job titles, no formal job descriptions, no organizational charts or departments. Everyone is cross-trained and encouraged to take initiative, resulting in innovative products and a motivated workforce.

There have been highly visible manufacturing companies in the region for some time. Tropicana, whose name is practically synonymous with orange juice, just celebrated its 60th anniversary. What began as

Sarasota boasts a wide range of manufacturing, from technology to kitchen cabinets.

PPi TECHNOLOGIES GLOBAL

ESTABLISHED 1996 **www.ppitechnologies.com**

PPi Technologies Global was started in 1996 by Stuart C. Murray. He wanted to sell both machinery and consumables as a 'total system' rather than selling just StandUp pouch machinery, which very often did not offer the customer the best solution. This approach resulted in a joint venture with Laudenberg of Germany, Nishibe/Altech Packaging Systems of Japan and Cellpack of Switzerland in a new company called **PROFILE®** **Packaging**. The company was formed to sell machinery that manufactures pouches with slider and press-to-close zippers from printed laminated roll stock films.

They also offer prefabricated pouches with spout fitments, a first for the North American market.

This was rapidly followed with financial investments with Leepack of Korea and exclusive distribution rights with Abtech of South Africa to offer prefabricated fill-seal StandUp pouch machinery through the aptly named **Pak*Source Global*** company.

In 2006, PLG Korea, PSG South Africa and PCG China offices were opened for trading within these countries offering USA industry standard machinery and pouch supplies from around the world. Over the years these strategic global partnerships

have set the standard for the StandUp pouch industry and helped the enormous growth of the StandUp pouch market. Today **PPi Technologies** Global is the largest supplier of StandUp pouch machinery in North America.

The ***PPi Technologies Global*** mission is to offer the best global StandUp pouch and tray solutions available, covering a full range from semi-automatic to high speed continuous motion machinery. **PouchPac Innovations** was formed to develop in-house patents and to market these technical features to their 'Fortune 500' customers and provide them the necessary market edge they needed.

An important part of the original business plan was not to just sell machines to customers, but to develop 21 markets covering for example, the food (including fresh and microwave), beverage, pet foods, healthcare and chemical segments amongst others.

R. Charles Murray, the Chief Executive Officer, stated, "The alcohol and beverage segment proved really challenging because of their traditional reliance on ridged bottles and cans. With much tenacity, we have been successful and watched with pride the recent introduction of water, juice, wine, cocktails, spirits and draft beer into StandUp pouches with many patented features around these new packages. This is the way forward for this industry in the 21st century."

PPi Technologies Global has won many awards over the past 12 years including #1 in the Florida Fast 50 and #139 in the National Fast 500 Technology Companies.

BUSY BEE CABINETS

ESTABLISHED 1982 www.busybeecabinets.com

Known for upscale kitchen and bathroom cabinetry design and manufacturing, Busy Bee Cabinets, Inc., is an unqualified success story. The privately owned company was founded in 1982 by Matt and Diana Uebelacker. They started out in Matt's father's

garage and made frame style cabinets to supply local builders. Now, twenty five years later, the owners can point to a new 40,000 square foot facility in North Port, encompassing three buildings, where much of the operation is streamlined and automated. Manufacturing an average of 200 units a day, the company has over 80 employees and a fleet of 27 trucks. In 2006, they generated $11 million in sales—representing an 18 percent increase over the previous year.

As a vertically integrated business, Busy Bee Cabinets, Inc. handles everything from sales and design to manufacturing and installation. Although core products are kitchen and bath cabinets, the company also creates home entertainment

centers, wall units, vanity cabinets, libraries, closets and home office desks and work stations, in addition to, offering a full warranty and service department.

With a reputation for innovation and a commitment to quality and service, Busy Bee Cabinets, Inc. is one of the fastest growing full service cabinet companies in Southwest Florida. Upon joining the Economic Development Corporation (EDC) of Sarasota County in 2006, the company won the prestigious "Manufacturer of the Year" Award for its pioneering approach and business strength.

Throughout its quarter century history, Busy Bee has primarily built kitchen and bathroom cabinets for major home builders and developers such as

Taylor Woodrow, U.S. Homes, Transeastern Homes and WCI. The company has installed its elegant products in venues from Tampa to Marco Island south of Naples.

In recent years the company has diversified to include sales and design for custom builders, home remodelers and private "do it yourself" home owners. The sales staff of seven, all with a minimum of 12 years of experience in the cabinet industry, knows how to design stylish thermofoil or hard wood cabinets for moderate and high-end homes ranging from $200,000 to $5 million. Using computer generated layouts that include floor plans, elevations and perspective views, the sales and design representatives can provide customers with a fully realized version of what their finished cabinets will look like in their present or future home.

To better serve the private sector and show off all the new products, the company recently remodeled and expanded its showroom in North Port. The 2,500 square foot state-of-the-art facility features a number of high-end concept kitchen, closet and door displays. Flat screen monitors throughout provide visitors with further examples and the variety of options in the field of cabinet styles and finishes Busy Bee can offer. A special "surface room" displays various counter top finishes, including quartz, granite, and cultured marble. Also featured are the fine lines of accessories the company carries in a vast array of colors, styles and finishes.

Because of its forward-looking owners, innovation is an essential part of the company. Known as a leader in the industry in engineering and construction methods, Busy Bee Cabinets, Inc. is always on the look-out for new manufacturing techniques. In addition to automating much of the cabinet assembly, it has recently created its own thermafoil finishing department,

where cabinet doors are laminated using a special heat treatment process.

With a commitment to innovation, quality and service, Busy Bee Cabinets, Inc. is looking to stay on the cutting edge. In the words of Matt Uebelacker, "Our vision for the future is for a strong and prosperous business built on our numerous successes."

143

L-3 COMMUNICATIONS

ESTABLISHED 1997 www.l-3ar.com

Located in the heart of Sarasota County, **L-3 Communications'** diverse business operations employ more than 400 technical and support professionals, in world-class engineering, manufacturing, sales, marketing, design and development of high technology products. The company is situated within a 150,000+ square foot facility in Sarasota, housing sophisticated capabilities within two distinct operations, Aviation Recorders (AR) and Medical Education Technologies, Inc. (METI).

On a global basis, **L-3 Communications** has grown quickly into the sixth largest defense company in the United States and is publicly traded on the NYSE (LLL). The company is a leader and prime defense contractor in intelligence, surveillance and reconnaissance, secure communications, government services, training and simulation, aircraft modernization and maintenance.

Our local L-3 **Aviation Recorders (AR)** Division has been a Sarasota mainstay for many years and has leveraged its 50 years of industry leading technology, expanding its product line to include avionics, transceivers, and instrumentation. Over the years, ownership of the product line has passed from Fairchild Camera Corporation to a number of other companies including Schlumberger, Loral,

Lockheed Martin, and **L-3 Communications**. Being part of L-3 since it was founded in April 1997, Aviation Recorders is the world's leading manufacturer of Solid State Cockpit Voice; Flight Data; and Maritime Voyage Recorders, Automatic Identification Systems; and Digital Selective Calling radios for multiple applications. As industry pioneers, L-3 AR products have set the standards for aviation and maritime data recorder technology, reliability, and survivability. L-3 is a Trustee member with The Greater Sarasota Chamber of Commerce and has made significant financial contributions to local organizations, including establishment of the USF Sarasota-Manatee campus.

Additionally, **Medical Education Technologies, Inc.® (METI®)** is the world's foremost provider of patient and surgical simulation technology and related educational software for health care education. Since its inception in 1996, thousands

of organizations worldwide are utilizing METI's technologies, including leading medical schools such as The Mayo Clinic, Harvard, Cornell, UCLA, Cleveland Clinic, Stanford and others. METI's unwavering dedication is to develop robust learning tools that meet and exceed the educational objectives of health care educators and learners alike. Pushing the envelope on realism, service and education has earned METI a distinct reputation in the industry and a loyal customer base devoted to the METI family mission: to save lives.

L-3 Communications continues its efforts to grow business operations and to be recognized as the Sarasota area's employer of choice.

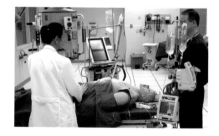

Many locally headquartered businesses have a national distribution.

a small fruit-packaging and fresh fruit salad business in Palmetto in 1947, is today, the world's largest fruit juice maker. Now owned by PepsiCo, it is Manatee County's second largest private company.

Chris-Craft, headquartered in Sarasota, is one of the world's most recognized names in leisure boats. Over the years, American presidents, business leaders and movie stars have owned the company's luxury boats for relaxation and fun. The distinctive looking hulls have become an American icon and have been featured in numerous Hollywood films and television shows. Indeed, in some dictionaries, Chris-Craft is listed as a synonym for pleasure boat.

The Tervis Tumbler Company has been making its popular plastic tumblers with its classic, retro look—one plastic cup sitting inside another—in Sarasota County since the 1960s when it moved here from Detroit, Michigan. In 2006, it opened a brand-new manufacturing

facility at the Triple Diamond Commerce Plaza in North Venice, where its distinctive logo is visible to anyone traveling on I-75. The show room, however, remains at the original location on U.S. 41 in Osprey.

What radically changed the manufacturing climate for the whole state, including the Sarasota-Manatee area, was Florida's deliberate and determined efforts to go high-tech. 1996, the Legislature established the Florida High Tech Corridor Council (FHTCC) to develop a strategic approach to attract high-tech companies. The unique partnership of universities, community colleges, local and regional economic development organizations and industry leaders in a 23 county belt from the east coast to the Gulf Coast across the center of the state has produced spectacular results.

In 2005, Florida was fourth among all states in high-tech job employment with a total of 276,400 workers, ranked second in number of new high-tech jobs added

JCI JONES CHEMICALS, INC.

ESTABLISHED 1930 **www.jcichemicals.com**

In 1930, John Wiley Jones, the founder of Sarasota based JCI Jones Chemicals, Inc., had a vision to create a company that would span the United States while at the same time have a positive impact upon the world. Perhaps he did not envision his company being one of the world's largest suppliers of water treatment chemicals for waste water.

In 1930, Mr. Jones began mixing substances in an old bathtub out in the garage of his upstate New York home. His background in chemistry guided him toward successfully producing a marketable product he later called Sunny Sol®. As the company grew, the product was distributed to grocery store chains

spanning the entire Northeastern United States.

By the 1940s, Jones had succeeded in building a network of distribution centers which saw further expansion during World War II. The company supplied the military across the United States

with the necessary chemicals to purify their own drinking water.

At the close of the war, this same distribution network propelled the company into further expansion as the needs of local municipalities in major cities were met.

From the 1950s through the present day, the company has continued to expand and refine its distribution network to meet the demands of a planet that continues to realize the essential need for pure drinking water and treated waste water.

Today, the company operates from 11 manufacturing and distribution centers spanning the United States. The Jones Family continues to own and operate the company privately, with Mr. Jones' grandchild, Jeffrey Jones as President and his great grandchildren Ryan and Jeffrey working in the corporate offices in Sarasota.

JCI is perhaps the largest seller of repackaged chlorine to municipal water authorities in most major cities and countries. Chlorine is considered to be the most effective means to insure the complete elimination of harmful microorganisms in water and to insure that water is pathogen free upon delivery to our nation's households and businesses. The pharmaceutical and paper industries also rely heavily upon JCI's products and services. JCI's export business has seen tremendous growth in the past 10 years, with accounts such as the Island Territories of Jamaica, Puerto Rico and the Dominican Republic.

JCI continues to be recognized by numerous awards for safe handling stewardship of the products handled by its employees and customers. The safety and security of its facilities is the primary area of focus for the company. The company has invested millions

in technological advancements, mitigation equipment and training to insure the protection of its facilities, transportation logistics, neighboring communities, customers and employees.

Throughout the company's long history is a dedication to support charitable organizations along with local communities. Today, as well as in the past, thousands of people across the country have benefited from the tens of millions of dollars donated by JCI during its long history. A full list of charities supported by JCI can be found on their website.

such an amazing success story of a man who dared to face the trials and tribulations of founding and establishing a great business. JCI will always look to the past to be reminded of the vision my grandfather began. I also truly appreciate the thousands of valued employees who enabled us to now be able to continue to look ahead to the significant opportunities we all have. Our goal is to continue on

Jeffrey Jones, President and C.E.O., remains convinced that the vision and teachings his grandfather established will long remain at JCI. "I feel truly blessed to be able to represent

with John Wiley Jones' success and keep alive the value he placed on safety, environmental stewardship and supporting the many worthwhile causes; truly helping those who are in need."

CRANE ENVIRONMENTAL

ESTABLISHED 1855 **www.cranenv.com**

Water is one of the most precious resources on the planet. Fresh water makes up less than 2% of all water on Earth and is increasingly scarce. Crane Environmental plays a vital role in increasing the supply of purified water for people and industry worldwide.

For more than 30 years, Crane Environmental has engineered and manufactured cutting-edge reverse osmosis systems that remove salt and other impurities from seawater, surface water, and aquifers. Its water purification systems are producing millions of gallons an hour in over 83 countries.

Headquartered in Venice, Crane Environmental provides jobs in a wide range of skill sets from engineering to assembly and fabrication. In addition to building advanced water treatment systems, Crane Environmental employees also utilize state-of-the-art lean manufacturing techniques to insure world-class customer service, operating performance, and quality.

Faster, Better, Easier!

Employees are empowered at all levels of the organization to identify ways to continuously improve all aspects of the business, from safety to sales growth. Employees also benefit from being part of our parent company, Crane Co.

Crane Co., (CR) NYSE, established over 150 years ago, is one of the oldest publicly held companies in the United States. It is also one of the ten most profitable companies of all time for its investors.

Timeless Ethics

Every internal Crane Co. presentation begins with the following statement by our founder, and it is the cornerstone of what we expect from ourselves as professionals:

"I am resolved to conduct my business in the strictest honesty and fairness; to avoid all deception and trickery; to deal fairly with both customers and competitors; to be liberal and just toward employees; and to put my whole mind upon the business." —Richard Teller Crane, 1855

Crane Environmentality™. Water is a precious resource, but it is not the only one. Crane Environmental adheres to an environmental policy that is good for the environment and even better for business.

By 2020, over two thirds of the world's population will be facing water shortages and Crane Environmental is ready to intervene with tomorrow's desalination equipment solutions. Our mission is to make sure that pure water is available and affordable for every generation to come.

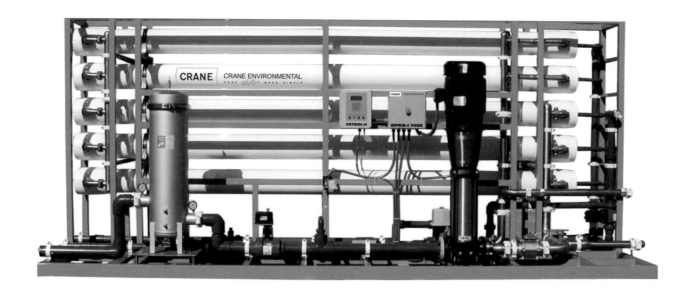

TELEFLEX ELECTRONICS

ESTABLISHED 1968 **www.teleflex.com**

Teleflex Electronics is an innovator of quality instrumentation since 1968, designs and manufacturers products for markets that demand quality, durability and performance. Teleflex creates a competitive edge for their customers where their proud manufacturing heritage merges with promising new technologies.

Teleflex Electronics, located in the Lakewood Ranch Corporate Park, has been a leading manufacturer of engine monitoring instrumentation for the marine, industrial, and heavy duty truck industries. The company started producing analog components that simply monitored and reported engine functions. Forty years later, they now produce information systems that not only monitor and report, but also control and protect vital engine systems by triggering alarms and shut-down procedures. Even today, Teleflex Electronics

extends its evolution through new product development.

By solving complex design and manufacturing challenges and maintaining the highest quality standards and procedures in the industry, Teleflex Electronics has earned preferred vendor status with many of their customers. Customers include such well-known companies as Caterpillar, Mercury Marine, Sea Ray, Chaparral, Honda, and John Deere. Innovation is integral to engineering and manufacturing. Internally, it drives Teleflex Electronics to build on their core technologies, to develop new products in which it has leadership and to find new applications for existing products. In partnership with clients, innovation adds value to the products sold to their customers!

In 1997, Teleflex Electronics moved to the Lakewood Ranch

Corporate Park, into their 83,000 air conditioned square foot facility, with state-of-the-art manufacturing capabilities, and future options for expanded growth. The current facility maintains manufacturing operations, as well as an Electronic Development Center. The facility is located off University Parkway, one of Sarasota's arterial roads to Interstate 75. Situated just two miles off the interstate and a short drive to downtown Sarasota, it is also located conveniently to the Sarasota Airport.

Teleflex Inc., the parent company, is a diversified company with global operations and customers worldwide. Teleflex is committed to an entrepreneurial spirit of creativity and innovation, building on new ideas and creating opportunities for profitable growth. Teleflex common stock is listed on the New York Stock Exchange (NYSE: TFX).

(10,900), and led the nation in the number of new high-tech establishments. Florida's high-tech exports grew by 13 percent or $1.4 billion in 2006. The total of $12.4 billion made Florida the third-largest technology exporting state in the nation.

As two of the 23 High Tech Corridor counties, Sarasota and Manatee Counties have their share of high-tech manufacturing and design companies. They include Eaton Corp., a Fortune 1000 aerospace company; Teltronics for telecommunications equipment; L-3

Sarasota was one of the first U.S. cities to offer universal Internet access to the public as a Wi-Fi "hot-zone."

Communications Aviation Recorders, the foremost maker of cockpit voice, flight data, and maritime voyage recorders; Hi-Stat Manufacturing, producers of temperature and speed sensors; and PGT Industries, the nation's leading manufacturer and supplier of residential impact-resistant windows and doors.

Also among the area's better kept secrets are specialty manufacturers that produce customized products for industries throughout the world. Sunset Mold & Prototype, Inc. makes high precision injection molds. JCI Jones Chemicals is one of the world's leading manufacturers and distributors of water treatment for municipal and industrial customers. Crane Environmental in Venice is a world leader in water purification. Teleflex, Inc. creates specialty engineered products for commercial, medical and aerospace industries.

Another growing sector is bio-science and medical equipment. Florida ranks second in the nation for the number of bio-science startups, and the Gulf Coast area continues to attract companies and research facilities. In Sarasota, DNA Print Genomics focuses on genetic testing products and services with clients in forensic science, genealogical research and pharmaceutical development. The Roskamp Institute in Bradenton does cutting edge research in Alzheimers' disease and head injuries, and conducts clinical trials for pharmaceutical companies. Aso Corporation is the world's largest producer of adhesive bandages and supplier of wound care products.

The High Tech Corridor initiatives also encourage interfaces and research partnerships between local universities and colleges and the technology arena. Several local high-tech companies utilize the facilities of USF in Tampa for research and development. The USF Sarasota-Manatee Leadership Council includes business and manufacturing leaders that represent 15 different industries and sectors. The council advises the university on program and service priorities that best serve the needs of the local market, which in turn contributes to the development of a highly skilled labor force for the area.

When downtown Sarasota became a Wi-Fi "hot zone" in 2005, it was one of the first cities in the U.S. to make wireless Internet access universally available to the public. The "Downtown Unplugged" initiative came about as the result of a partnership between the Sarasota County

THE BOAR'S HEAD DIFFERENCE

ESTABLISHED 2001 **www.boarshead.com**

Manufacturer of premium delicatessen meats and cheeses cares about quality, community and employees.

A Home in Sarasota

Boar's Head Provisions Co., Inc. came to sunny Sarasota, Florida in 2001, after calling New York home for just over 95 years. The move proved to be an inspired choice, not just for the warm weather, but for furthering a growing relationship with Publix Super Markets, located in nearby Lakeland, Florida. While 2,400 Boar's Head and sister company Frank Brunckhorst Co., LLC employees continue to work at facilities in New York, New Jersey, Michigan, Arkansas, and Virginia, Sarasota is now the headquarters, housing 138 employees. Boar's Head supports a variety of charities and organizations, because not only do the employees work hard, they also care about the community. You'll find them serving product, walking long miles or making donations to the Salvation Army, Sarasota Little League, Juvenile Diabetes Research, Relay for Life or the Humane Society, to name just a few. Boar's Head is also a proud contributor to enduring Sarasota institutions like the Shrine Circus and the Van Wezel Performing Arts Center.

Boar's Head History

The first products were distributed under the Boar's Head name in New York in 1905. They were delivered by horse-drawn wagon to small delicatessens, and soon distribution had grown significantly. It was then that founder Frank Brunckhorst, dissatisfied with the quality of available product, opened his own manufacturing plant in a small Brooklyn building. The products came into demand, and before long Boar's Head had made its way into the best New York delicatessens. By the mid 1970's, requests were coming from across the country, and now the freshest products are delivered via distributors to retailers in 48 states.

Quality Meats & Cheeses

Using only pure beef, poultry, and pork, and real spices, Boar's Head has continued to maintain the unwavering standards of quality set over a century ago, never using by-products, cereals, fillers, artificial flavors or colors. Through the years, while other manufacturers have made compromises, Boar's Head has kept quality a top priority, even starting a deli school to teach proper product care. It's this passion for perfection that drives each employee, and for these reasons, many of America's most prestigious, quality-conscious stores stake their reputation on the Boar's Head Brand and the amazing array of over 300 products that bear the name, Boar's Head.

government and 82 Degrees Tech, a technology advocacy group, whose mission is to increase public awareness of the growing private technology sector in the region and to further the business climate by developing resources essential to high-tech development. Plans are in the works to utilize WiMAX wireless technology to expand the coverage for wireless Internet access to all of Sarasota and Manatee Counties.

For other high-speed Internet access, Comcast of West Florida, the main cable company in the area, offers a basic tier speed of 6 Mbps (megabits per second) and a premium tier speed of 8 Mbps, and plans further speed increases in the future. Verizon, the dominant telephone service, delivers fiber-optic and digital-optic capabilities to all industrial and commercial zones in Sarasota County. In 2005, the company started to lay a network of new fiber-optic cables—"fiber to the premises" (FTTP) technology—that can deliver greater bandwidth and download speeds of up to 30 Mbps for its next-generation FIOS Internet access, voice and video applications.

Thus, the region, which has one of the highest concentrations of personal computer owners in the world, is well ahead of the curve when it comes to the latest technology advances in telecommunication for both businesses and residents.

business
& services

business
& services

WHETHER YOU'RE AN ENTREPRENEUR PLANNING TO start a brand-new business, a major company looking to relocate, or an existing area business aiming to expand, Sarasota is a great place to find excellent support, satisfaction and success. The combination of forward-looking business leadership, modern technology and infrastructure, a highly educated workforce, moderate taxes and financial incentives has positioned the area in the forefront of meeting

the challenges of a global economy. Because of Sarasota's scenic location and history as a vacation and retirement paradise, tourist and service industries, including hotels, restaurants and retail outlets, predominate in the local economy. In 2005, total retail sales for the Sarasota-Bradenton-Venice MSA reached $9.8 billion.

At the same time, art and culture occupy an important part of the overall economic picture.

A comprehensive study of Sarasota's nonprofit arts industry revealed that the arts generated more than $122 million every year, generating 2,956 full-time equivalent jobs, providing $83 million in resident household income, yielding $5.6 million in local government tax revenues and $9 million in state government revenues. Sarasota is also emerging as a leading community for doing business in the 21st century. In 2003, *Forbes* magazine ranked Sarasota

Local and regional organizations have helped to create economic growth and a healthy business climate.

County the 44th "Best Place to Live and Do Business" out of the largest 150 U.S. cities. *BizJournal* named Sarasota-Bradenton the second best market to grow a small business nationwide in 2007. In fact, Sarasota County outpaces the state and the nation in growth of employees, payroll and firms.

A number of companies already take advantage of the region's business-friendly climate. There are more than 40 national and international corporate headquarters in the Sarasota area, including FCCI Insurance Group, Boar's Head Provisions, Sun Hydraulics Corporation, Scott Paint Company and Bealls department stores. In addition, a number of prominent companies, such as Honeywell, Nielsen Media Research and Forest Products Supply take advantage of all the benefits for doing business here. According to the *Expansion Management* magazine, Sarasota-Bradenton ranks in the Top 20 Large Metros for business recruitment and attraction (out of 362 nationwide).

The area is well served by local, national and Fortune 100 companies. Publix Super Markets, Inc., the dominant grocery chain in Florida, is also Sarasota County's largest private employer, followed by Wal-Mart

and FCCI Insurance Group. Other major national chain stores well represented throughout the region include Target, Home Depot, Lowe's, Office Depot and Winn-Dixie supermarkets.

The economic success is hardly accidental. Sarasota and Manatee Counties have deliberate strategies to encourage economic growth. Both have developed a number of local and regional organizations that have been instrumental in creating an outstanding business climate.

Business leaders are involved in educational initiatives, such as the USF Sarasota-Manatee Leadership Council, which advises the university how to best serve the needs of the local market. SCOPE (Sarasota County Openly Plans for Excellence) is a forum that provides dialogue and impartial research on many important social, environmental and economic issues confronting the community. With a board of directors composed of leaders from nonprofit, education, business, government, youth and civic organizations, SCOPE seeks to establish priorities, propose solutions and monitor change in order to enhance the quality of life in the area.

FCCI INSURANCE GROUP

ESTABLISHED 1959 www.fcci-group.com

FCCI's corporate headquarters in Lakewood Ranch

FCCI was started in 1959 by a group of Sarasota businessmen who wanted to self-insure to save money on the cost of workers' compensation insurance. Today, FCCI uses independent agents and a regional focus to provide comprehensive property and casualty coverage throughout the Southeast and Midwest.

Over the years, FCCI has grown with the community— from a handful of employees in 1959 to more than 670 today; from $52,000 in premium to more than $551 million; from 28 fund members to over 15,000 policyholders.

Locally, FCCI kept outgrowing its facilities and moved from South Pineapple to North Lemon, to a converted house on South Tamiami Trail, to a three-story building on Mound Street, then to a five-story building on Cattlemen Road, and finally, in 2001, to a 260,000 square-foot, state-of-the-art facility on University Parkway in Lakewood Ranch.

FCCI's mission is to provide commercial property and casualty insurance products to fulfill the needs of their independent agents and policyholders in the markets they serve today and those they will enter in the future. As part of this mission, FCCI will expand in an orderly fashion and on a profitable basis to increase their capability for fulfilling their customers' needs and to provide a quality market for the products they sell.

Customer service has always been a top priority at FCCI. In addition, all the company's efforts are guided by a continuing commitment to the highest ethical values and integrity. Loyalty, integrity, vision, excellence, and service are the core values that guide FCCI employees every day.

FCCI's corporate culture creates opportunities for employees to get involved and make a difference. Thanks to the employees' generous donations and volunteerism, many worthwhile charities have the support necessary to reach out and help those in need.

In 2009, FCCI will celebrate its 50th anniversary. As a leader in the commercial property and casualty industry, FCCI is proud of its Sarasota heritage and proud to be recognized as the First Choice in Commercial Insurance.

ALVIN J. SINGLETON, INC. ROOFING CONTRACTORS

ESTABLISHED 1969 www.singletonroofing.com

Singleton Roofing began in 1969 when Orzel Singleton decided there was a better way to treat customers by bringing expert roofing knowledge, honesty and integrity of doing business to fellow Sarasotans. This would become the cornerstone of his business.

When the time came for his son, Alvin, to take over the company, he continued his father's philosophy and now more than 35 years later, treating customers with fairness and respect are second nature. This sound moral foundation allows Singleton Roofing to grow and Alvin has been a positive influence in the Sarasota area. From homes in Lakewood Ranch to Longboat Key to Venice, it is difficult to find a Sarasota neighborhood where Singleton Roofing has not had a project.

The company supports many local organizations, such as Miss Sarasota Softball, Newtown Baseball, and Girls, Inc. Youth charities are not the only beneficiaries of his involvement as Alvin also serves as a Past-President and is an active member of the Sarasota Manatee Roofing and Sheet Metal Contractors Association.

Alvin believes strongly in constant improvement. Knowledge gained through membership in the National Roofing Contractors Association as well as the Florida Roofing and Sheet Metal Contractors Association, allows Singleton Roofing to learn and use the industry's best practices and apply them to Sarasota's roofs.

As Singleton Roofing has grown so has its family involvement. A third generation now helps to ensure the high standards remain in place since the company's inception. Throughout the course of almost four decades, Singleton Roofing has honored the people of Sarasota with quality, honesty, service, and fairness.

Singleton Roofing has a comprehensive website where new and current residents can find information on commercial or residential roofing, new construction, re-roofing and repairs, as well as roofing products.

BENDERSON DEVELOPMENT COMPANY, LLC

ESTABLISHED 1952 **www.benderson.com**

*Developing University
Town Center*

With over 55 years of experience, Benderson Development Company, LLC has engineered impressive growth through innovation, insight and determination. The company's expertise in shopping center development has led to substantial growth throughout the country. Operating in over 35 states, Benderson owns and manages over 540 properties encompassing over 35 million square feet of leasable space, which make it one of the largest privately owned development companies in North America. Benderson's development portfolio includes retail centers, office buildings, industrial parks, residential communities, hotels and apartment complexes.

In 1940, Nathan Benderson purchased an old courthouse in Buffalo, New York that launched his career into real estate and would eventually evolve into the Benderson Development Company. One of the company's early projects was the nation's first open-air shopping centers anchored by a supermarket. A few decades later, the company opened the Niagara Factory Outlet Mall, which was one of the first outlet malls in the country. Today, the youngest of his three sons, Randy Benderson, is the managing director of Benderson Development and oversees the

Randy Benderson with his father and company founder, Nathan, his son, Shaun, and their buffalo mascot in front of their Sarasota, Florida headquarters.

day-to-day operations of the company along with his son Shaun.

Relocating its corporate headquarters to Sarasota, Florida in 2003, the company has actively begun working on one of its largest projects to date in University Town Center. When completed, University Town Center will be the premier mixed-use shopping center development in southwest Florida. The project will encompass approximately 1.9 million square feet of world-class shopping destinations, office buildings, hotels and over 1,700 residential units at the southwest corner of Interstate 75 and University Parkway.

The entire site, designed by the premier new urbanism architect in the country—Moule & Polyzoides, will be built around a walk able, pedestrian friendly environment complete with natural open spaces and a community park.

At the epicenter of the town center project, will be an unmatched shopping center destination featuring distinctive design and dramatic architecture. Guests will be able to enjoy the finest collection of specialty stores, restaurants and entertainment destinations including the region's only Nordstrom's Department Store.

Super Target, the anchor for Phase I of the project, opened with tremendous success in October 2006. Phase II of the mixed-use project will commence in the fall of 2007 with a grand opening currently scheduled to occur by the end of 2009.

Custom Residence

SRQ: Sarasota's Premier Magazine (*SRQ Magazine*) Home of the Year Award Platinum Winner 2004

Situated on two-plus acres, this 3,200 square-foot Sarasota residence was designed to reflect the client's desire for a minimalist home in which they could equally live and entertain. The concept of the layout was to create a separation of these functions with architectural elements but to tie the design together with light, form and repetition.

Feature articles on the custom family home appeared in: *Sarasota Herald-Tribune*; *SRQ Magazine*; *Dream Homes of Florida*; *Perspectives on Design*

JONATHAN PARKS ARCHITECT

ESTABLISHED 2001   www.jpa-architect.com

Design, in its purest form, fulfills functional and aesthetic requirements completely, elegantly and economically. JONATHAN PARKS ARCHITECT (JPA) has emerged as one of the fastest growing architecture and design firms in Florida, focusing on one essential ideal— that great design can change the way that people live. From new construction to historical restoration, from luxury residences to large-scale commercial projects, JPA provides comprehensive services in planning, architecture, interior design, and graphic design.

The diverse team of multi-talented designers at JPA works with authenticity, purpose and balance. The firm encourages client interaction throughout the course of design and provides distinctive, timeless solutions that uniquely fit the client's needs.

JPA offers comprehensive services in **planning** and site development. A unique appreciation for not just buildings, but also the spaces between buildings gives JPA an added advantage in creating successful, pedestrian-oriented mixed use environments

Historic Restoration

H. Dean Rowe, FAIA Award for Design Excellence 2007
Tampa Bay Association of the American Institute of Architects

Honor Award in Historic Preservation 2007
Tampa Bay Association of the American Institute of Architects

First Place Award for Interior Rehabilitation 2005
National Trust for Historic Preservation and Old-House
Journal sponsored Great American Home Awards

Paul Rudolph designed this award winning Modernist
"Sarasota style" home in 1954 for David and Eleene Cohen.
The home was purchased by Jerry and Beverly Vross from the
Cohens who restored and updated it themselves with the help
and guidance of architect Jonathan Parks. The interior and the
exterior were restored using the standards of the National Trust
for Historic Preservation as the guidelines.

Feature articles on the Cohen House appeared in:
Robb Report Vacation Home; *Preservation Magazine*;
Old-House Journal; *SRQ Magazine*; *Sarasota Herald-Tribune*

that transform commonplace areas into thriving centers of urban and neighborhood activity.

JPA creates dynamic **architecture** centered on the unique aspects of each project and client, residential and commercial. Known for its clarity of concept and quality of work, JPA has received national and regional awards in architecture, design and restoration. Jonathan Parks AIA credits the firm's success to a highly skilled, uncompromising team and to great clients dedicated to the same principle of creating great architecture that serves as a background for changing the way people live and work.

Together with the architecture staff, JPA's **interior design** department ensures that from a project's inception through completion, a building's basic concept is reflected in the design of its interiors. JPA helps clients strategize, plan, and design their space to successfully define how people interact with each other and their environment.

JPA parallels its other disciplines with an innovative **graphic design** department. The firm offers a full spectrum of graphic services tailored to the needs of the client.

With JPA a client can achieve a complete image from site aesthetics, building design, and interior interface to branding. The architects and designers of JPA believe that creating timeless and elegant designs in planning, architecture, interior design, and graphic design ensures that the client's goals are fully realized.

DooleyMack Constructors headquarters in Lakewood Ranch.

DOOLEYMACK CONSTRUCTORS

ESTABLISHED 1977 **www.dooleymack.com**

William R. Dooley and Kenneth D. Smith were childhood friends, who never imagined their paths would cross later in life to create a business. In 1977, DooleyMack Constructors opened its doors, with Wendy Mack, CFO, joining the team shortly thereafter. Today, the Lakewood Ranch based business is ranked 4th in the "Top 50 Contractors" by *Gulf Coast Business Review* and is ranked in the "Top 400 Contractors 2006" by *Engineering News Record*. As quoted by Senator Bob Johnson, "DooleyMack represents the finest construction firm in southwest Florida, their competitive spirit, diligence and workmanship have brought them excellent reviews and acclaim." Today, the DooleyMack team has more than 180 associates, with offices located in Fort Lauderdale, Panama City, Key West, Atlanta, Dallas and the Carolinas. DooleyMack provides services to the following core markets: condo/multi-family, healthcare, education, hospitality, commercial, retail and historical restoration. DooleyMack offers specialized services in: construction management, pre-construction services, general contracting, program management, design/build, master planning and development.

DooleyMack's portfolio includes the historic Sarasota Courthouse, and award winning Florida landmarks including: the restoration of Ruebens Gallery at Ringling Museum, Van Wezel Performing Arts Theater, World War II Barracks in Jupiter, the Cape Florida Lighthouse, the Jupiter Inlet Lighthouse and the structural restoration of Fort Zachary Taylor.

In 2006, The Association of Builders and Contractors awarded DooleyMack the Excellence in Construction Award for the Charlotte County Schools Hurricane Recovery Project for completing two modular campuses, Punta Gorda Middle School and Charlotte County High School.

A business is only as good as its associates, and DooleyMack actively recruits talent from local schools and colleges, encouraging students to explore construction and technical trades from a young age. As an integral part of the community, DooleyMack is involved in many area organizations, and is proud to call Sarasota home.

DooleyMack believes, "people do business with people" that they like and trust. They focus on delivering impeccable workmanship, valuable services and long-term relationships, resulting in 80% repeat business and client referrals. The company is a progressive organization dedicated to construction excellence and building relationships with lasting value.

At the regional level, 82Degrees Tech, a private sector advocacy group, raises awareness about technology issues and pushes to expand the area's state-of-the-art technology capacity and infrastructure. Sarasota and Manatee Counties are members of the Tampa Bay Partnership, a regional economic organization that seeks to stimulate economic growth and development via corporate relocation and business expansion. At the same time, both counties belong to Florida High Tech Corridor Council, whose mission is to attract, retain and grow high-tech companies within a 23 county sector by partnering with research facilities at colleges and universities.

Both Sarasota and Manatee Counties have active Chambers of Commerce and Economic Development Corporations (EDCs), which offer a host of programs to encourage businesses to flourish. They assist existing companies with plans for expansion, solicit new businesses for the area, and promote the counties' business image. There are also active Chambers of Commerce in Venice, Englewood and North Port.

Companies seeking to expand or relocate can count on a large, well-educated labor force. Nearly half of Sarasota County's population is within the prime working age range of 25 to 64. That equates to a workforce of 160,000. Adding in the neighboring Manatee and Charlotte Counties, the region has 350,000 workers at the disposal of business and industry.

Outstanding schools and significant research and education facilities ensure that the area's labor force is highly skilled and well educated. According to 2005 U.S. Census Bureau figures, Sarasota County leads Florida and the U.S. in percentage of high school graduates and adults with bachelor's degrees or higher. More than half of working adults over the age of 25 have continued their education at the college level and beyond.

Workforce development is such a priority in Sarasota County that the EDC employs a specialist whose primary focus is workforce assistance. A recruitment assistance program offers access to a free database where local employers can post job openings. In addition, those looking for work can also post their resume online. Young professionals being recruited by Sarasota or Manatee businesses can also make use of a one-stop resource center online to help with relocation. Supported by both county's EDCs, www.southtampabay.org

Corporations enjoy outstanding views and convenient interstate access.

APAC

ESTABLISHED 1900 **www.apac.com**

The Southern Florida Division of APAC® is a leading provider of high-quality asphalt paving services, construction aggregate and asphalt hot mix sales. The Division specializes in public, private and commercial construction including earthwork, road building and asphalt paving. The Southern Florida Division has the expertise and ability to complete large road construction projects and resurfacing paving projects on time and within budget.

APAC, one of the largest U.S. highway contractors has been at the forefront of innovation in the paving industry for more than 120 years, having paved the first asphalt road in America in 1879, and received the first patent for bitulithic paving in 1900. Today, APAC, a subsidiary of Oldcastle Materials Group, is a network of divisions operating in the Southeastern and Midwestern states. APAC has the financial strength and bonding capacity to construct large projects, as well as the local presence, commitment and desire to perform small projects.

"Commitment to Excellence" is the title of APAC's Environmental, Health and Safety (EHS) Plan. This commitment is the very foundation of this unique approach to safety. Employees work together to make safety everyone's responsibility. The "Beyond Compliance" philosophy is so pervasive that it lifts the EHS program to an intensity, resource and investment level unparalleled in this industry. As with many major employers, employees are the most valuable asset. Safety at APAC is the core value, and environmental stewardship is imperative, and APAC's EHS program and safety culture is second to none.

APAC's talented, dedicated and experienced employees distinguish themselves from the industry. The company's reputation, stability and career opportunities attract the best candidates. New employees are trained and continue to learn by working with management whose average length of service with APAC is 15 years. This level of experience assures the customer, that only the highest-caliber, most talented professionals will be building their projects.

APAC has been an integral part of Sarasota County and is committed to the supply of Hot Mix Asphalt or the delivery of construction projects on time, on budget and with complete satisfaction. The company is proud of their people and of their work. Understand that each road, bridge, highway and parking lot built stands as a testament to APAC's commitment to safety, quality, performance and customer satisfaction.

MULLET'S APPLIANCES

ESTABLISHED 1974 www.mullets.com

Where Style Meets Function

Since 1974, Mullet's Appliances has successfully exceeded customers' expectations by offering quality products and unparalleled personal service. Whenever clients are looking to create that dream kitchen, rest assured that Mullet's will deliver these dreams to their doorstep. As a family-owned and operated business, Mullet's is dedicated to treating customers like family by offering diverse products and luxury lines with competitive prices, coupled with honest, professional service. Understand that when building a home or remodeling a kitchen, the decision-making process can be difficult. With a friendly and knowledgeable sales team they are committed to helping clients select the perfect appliances to not only meet functional needs, but to create a desirable elite and trend-setting kitchen.

Mullet's Appliances offers renowned brands such as KitchenAid, Subzero, Thermador, Viking, Whirlpool, Wolf, plus many more. Designing a dramatic kitchen with both style and function is a science that Mullet's professionals have mastered. With impeccable selection and reliable reputation, Mullet's has fulfilled clients' kitchen needs, taking them through every step and decision with intelligence and poise.

Mullet's is multi-faceted, not only in sales and products, but

also in service. Skilled staff of certified technicians and a full-service parts department, stand ready to assist customers with any needs that may arise in the future. As an industry leader, Mullet's family of clientele, have grown to expect service, not only today but for the life of their appliances.

With more than 30 years of servicing Sarasota and Manatee counties, Mullet's Appliances continues to excel in integrity and excellence—a must in today's demanding marketplace.

Mullet's Appliances has two locations: the main sales center located on Clark Road in Sarasota and a second branch at Trade Center Way in Naples. The newest addition to the Clark Road showroom is a Subzero-Wolf *Living Kitchen* display.

Consumers have enjoyed the cutting-edge technology in luxury appliances, displayed in aesthetic kitchen vignettes, enabling clients to envision different appliances in real-life settings.

As a major retailer of premier brands of luxury appliances, Mullet's Appliances has defined themselves by the satisfied customer, ever mindful that through dedicated employees exceeding industry standards, this company continues to grow not only in product quality but by unmatched service, selection and value.

SUNSET AUTOMOTIVE GROUP

ESTABLISHED 1979 **www.sunsetautogroup.com**

When longtime residents of Sarasota ask who Sunset Automotive Group is, the answer is usually Sunset Chevrolet or Sunset Dodge. They would only be partially right. Sunset Automotive Group really began in Sarasota over 28 years ago when Robert Geyer had the opportunity to purchase a local Chevrolet dealership and rename it Sunset. At the time, he owned and operated a successful Chevrolet dealership in Miami. After traveling back and forth for a while, he decided Sarasota was the place he wanted to not only raise his family, but grow his business.

Robert Geyer, President of the Sunset Automotive Group, began his career as a banker at M&T Bank in Buffalo, New York. It was there as a loan officer Geyer had the opportunity to purchase into Central Chevrolet in Springfield, Massachusetts

in January of 1967. Three years later, he sold his interest in that dealership and purchased Tropical Chevrolet in Miami.

In November 1979, an opportunity in Sarasota presented itself and he has never looked back. Geyer has remained focused on building what is now considered the strongest independent automobile group in southwest Florida— Sunset Automotive Group.

Today, after more than 28 years of sustained growth, Sunset Automotive Group now consists of 16 different automotive franchises at 12 locations. They also employ over 650 people from our surrounding communities.

Geyer purchased a Dodge franchise in 1985, renaming it Sunset Dodge. One year later in partnership with Patrick H. Dickinson, a local attorney and longtime resident

of Sarasota, Coast Cadillac was purchased followed in rapid succession by Crest Cadillac (1988), Tropical Cadillac (1990), Coast Volvo (1992), Saturn of Manatee (1992), Saturn of Sarasota (1995), Coast Infiniti (1997), Sunset Pontiac (1997), Suncoast Porsche Audi VW (1999), and Suncoast Kia (2001). The next group to be purchased was Sunset Suzuki (2003), Sunset Jeep Subaru Mitsubishi (2004) and most recently, Sunset Buick (2006). Each store is within fifteen miles from the beginning store, Sunset Chevrolet, where Mr. Geyer still has his office and can be found staying involved and working with consumers and community needs.

Sunset's growth is due to strong leadership and understanding customers' needs. The company's mission statement is "It is the mission of the Sunset Automotive Group to encourage our employees to reach their full potential and thereby create customers who have confidence that our team professionally exceeds their individual expectations so that they will remain loyal to our brand and organization."

Since its establishment, the Sunset Automotive Group has been dedicated to providing the very best in automotive sales, service, parts, and collision repair to the communities that they serve in Bradenton, Sarasota, and Venice. The Sunset Automotive Group name is synonymous with good business and satisfied customers.

Several of the dealerships have been recognized for excellence in their brand. All of the Cadillac stores have received the coveted Master Dealer award for excellence in sales and customer satisfaction. For twenty years Sunset Dodge has been ranked a Five Star Daimler Chrysler store, the highest recognition a Chrysler store can receive. Sunset Subaru has received the Stellar Performer reward and Suncoast Kia was honored with the Circle of Excellence award. Sunset Buick Pontiac was recently recognized with the Mark of Excellence award in 2006 and their Service Department was given the Best of the Best award. Other Sunset Automotive Group dealerships have been honored with achievement awards in all areas and are recognized throughout Florida's West Coast for dependability and integrity.

The Sunset Automotive Group has been equally impressive with contributions of time, money and resources to the community and charitable organizations. In 2007, Robert Geyer celebrated 40 years of contribution not only to the automotive business, but also to his commitment to numerous organizations throughout his career. Geyer presently serves on the Board of Trustees at Sarasota Memorial Healthcare Foundation and on the Board of Directors for the Salvation Army. He has been an active member of Church of the Palms since coming to Sarasota as an Elder chairing Building and Financial campaigns, in addition to teaching Sunday School.

The employees of Sunset Automotive Group are also extremely involved in the communities in which they live. They are active in local churches, charitable organizations, schools and other non-profits. Many serve on Boards throughout the area. In addition, each individual dealership sponsors a charity during the holidays where all the employees work together to lend a helping hand to those in the community in need.

The Sunset Automotive Group has a long history of community involvement and concern...it's just one more way for Sunset Automotive Group to encourage people to reach their full potential and make Sarasota a better community!

Many business parks can be found throughout the County.

offers information about careers, education, housing and recreational opportunities throughout the two-county area.

To meet the physical needs of business, Sarasota has a wide variety of venues throughout the county, from office space to warehousing to light manufacturing sites. Existing industrial and office building space as well as properties for new facilities are available in sizes ranging from 2,000 to 300,000 square feet.

Class A, B and C office space in downtown Sarasota includes high-rise office buildings, street level store fronts and work downstairs-live upstairs properties. Downtown Venice provides most of its available office space in picturesque Mediterranean-style one and two-story buildings. To the south, North Port is rolling out the carpet for business expansion. In 2005, it had more than 1 million square feet of commercial real estate under construction, much of it office space, in the planning stages.

A number of business parks throughout the county offer combinations of office, warehouse, distribution, manufacturing and flex space. In 2005, the county had 6.3 million square feet of leaseable user space, many of them technology capable, with a vacancy rate of 6 percent. Verizon Smart Parks include areas such as Cattleridge Business Center, Gateway Sarasota, Kane Plaza, Lakewood Ranch Corporate Park, North Port Park of Commerce, Palmer Park of Commerce and Sarasota City Center.

For companies and businesses wishing to expand and relocate to Sarasota County, there are incentives and support programs. The EDC can help find appropriate sites and buildings through its comprehensive database of available properties in the county. Compiled with

OSPREY REAL ESTATE SERVICES

ESTABLISHED 1999 **www.ospreymanagement.com**

Osprey is a diverse company with many interests including Osprey Real Estate Services and Osprey Management Company. As a full-service real estate company with an extensive portfolio of Class "A," Suburban Office, Medical Office, Flex & Industrial/Warehouse space and Golf properties, Osprey endeavors to seek out the best investments and the most efficient ways of managing these investments for their clients. They offer professional real estate services for various Osprey holding companies and partnerships as well as third-party clients in Florida, Michigan, and the Southeast United States, and its leading presence is dedicated to providing the best alternatives for its clients' varying space needs. With approximately 4,000,000 square feet of office and industrial property in its portfolio, Osprey Real Estate Services and Osprey Management Company directly handle all acquisitions, management and leasing internally. Their acquisition strategy includes targeting properties in Michigan, Florida and North Carolina as well as various other locations in the U.S. The company can provide expansion space as their tenants grow, whether by providing additional space in its large portfolio or a custom build-to-suit building.

Sarasota assets include Class "A" office space such as the Sarasota City Center, a 13-story, 248,000 square foot luxury high-rise in the heart of downtown Sarasota; the Live Oak Business Park and Cattleridge Business Park; and the 9000 Town Center Parkway building in Lakewood Ranch.

Osprey Construction & Development can provide the building solutions to help your development project succeed, with expertise spanning the full spectrum of general construction services from conceptual planning and preliminary budget preparations, through approvals and project design, to the ultimate construction of the project. Its portfolio of project work and offerings includes residential and mixed-use developments as well as office parks and golf properties.

Osprey Recreational Properties, formed in 2003 to acquire and operate quality golf-related properties, now has a portfolio of highly regarded golf facilities in Michigan, which include the Black Forest and Wilderness Valley Golf Courses near Gaylord, the Manistee National Golf & Resort near Manistee, the Medalist Golf Club near Marshall and the Ridgeview Golf Course near Kalamazoo.

R.E. CRAWFORD CONSTRUCTION

ESTABLISHED 1979 **www.recrawford.com**

Founded in 1979, R.E. Crawford Construction, with full-service locations in Sarasota, FL and Pittsburgh, PA, has become an important provider of construction services throughout the U.S. Their success has been credited to their ability to provide site development, ground-up and addition/renovation services to a wide range of clients. Ranked as one of the nation's top builders and renovators of retail and restaurant space, they have completed thousands of projects in the U.S. and Puerto Rico. In addition to retail and restaurant construction, R.E. Crawford serves hospitality, healthcare, institutional, commercial, light industrial, educational, warehousing and distribution

clients. Licensed in 43 states, the R.E. Crawford team has earned an excellent reputation that awards the company with repeat work from many of the nation's top companies: The Home Depot, Sheetz, AmeriSuites, Friendly's, Eat n' Park, Chick-Fil-A, Horizon Bank, Rite-Aid, Hilton Homewood Suites and Verizon Wireless.

The expertise of the professional field and management staff gives the company the flexibility to provide a variety of construction services. Using the general contracting and construction management, the R.E. Crawford Construction company is recognized for its ability to control costs, perform top quality work and meet the most demanding of schedules.

R.E. Crawford's team approach as well as their involvement in the preliminary planning stages allows them to balance design aesthetics with budget realities. Their conceptual evaluation is an effective tool to establish an accurate cost projection and their value engineering process has enabled several of their clients to recognize substantial savings on multimillion-dollar projects.

The R. E. Crawford Construction team of construction professionals brings considerable skill and experience to every project they undertake. They have been able to attract and maintain some of the best talent available in the industry. The organization and employees are committed to completing each assignment on schedule and within budget while maintaining an unsurpassed level of quality and customer service.

PURMORT & MARTIN
INSURANCE AGENCY, LLC

www.purmort.com

ESTABLISHED 1958

An Insurance Tradition For Five Generations

Independent insurance agencies pride themselves on serving their customers first and being able to offer a variety of quality

insurance products from a multiple selection of excellent companies. Adhering to this philosophy for over half a century, the owners and employees of Purmort & Martin Insurance have achieved outstanding results. The agency is consistently rated "The Best Insurance Agent" in the *Sarasota Herald-Tribune* Readers Poll, and it has become one of the area's largest locally owned, independent Insurance Agencies.

The employees and owners of the firm do not take this honor lightly, but strive to maintain this reputation by providing independent business owners and individuals with professional advice on insurance products that

meet their special needs. They build long-term relationships with their clients, based on mutual understanding, integrity and trust; and provide fast, accurate response to their requests with a high level of personal service.

The agency services and sells almost all forms of insurance, including commercial, personal and life policies. It is proud to include among its clients many of the area's leading businesses and individuals.

Just as the Purmort family has been an integral part of the insurance industry for five

generations, Purmort & Martin Insurance has been an integral part of the Sarasota community. The owners, Russ Bobbitt, Rick Martin, Jamie Purmort, and Matt Stepulla, as well as manager Wells Purmort, have an outstanding record of leadership in many area non profit organizations.

They have also been active on boards and committees in the insurance industry, including Florida Association of Independent Agents, Professional Insurance Agents of Florida, Sarasota Independent Insurance Agents Association, Cincinnati Insurance Company Presidents Club, CNA National PACER Advisory and Sarasota Insurance Women's Association.

The agency services the West Coast of Florida from its modern downtown Sarasota offices on Ringling Blvd. Their comprehensive website includes information about the agency along with their insurance underwriter partners. You will also find information for up to the minute hurricane information, hurricane preparedness steps and claims assistance information. In addition to the insurance company claims contacts and numbers can also be found.

JOHN CANNON HOMES, INC.

ESTABLISHED 1997 **www.johncannonhomes.com**

The Fine Art of Home Building

For over 20 years, John Cannon Homes, Inc., has set the standard in luxury custom home building and design, creating distinctive homes for people who appreciate the fine art of living well. Exquisite craftsmanship, uncompromising quality, the finest materials, and unparalleled personal service are the hallmarks of their success. Creating homes of timeless beauty and lasting value has earned John Cannon Homes the recognition of local and national awards year after year. The company's greatest reward, however, is the trust of home owners like you.

The John Cannon Homes Story

From an early age, building tree forts for his friends, John Cannon had a calling to build. After earning a degree in building construction from Michigan State University, he moved to Sarasota, Florida, to work as a management trainee for a national builder. Quickly moving up the ranks, he began overseeing projects on Florida's east coast. Soon, John returned to Sarasota where he met and married his wife, Phillipa. Almost immediately after starting their life together, they began a home-building business in their garage.

Today, with more than 100 projects a year, John Cannon Homes is considered one of Florida's premier builders, creating open, free-flowing floor plans and beautiful architectural designs. John Cannon Home's commitment to quality has been recognized through numerous awards. The company has consistently been voted Sarasota's "Best Builder" by the readers of the *Sarasota Herald-Tribune* and has also been the recipient of many other local and national awards.

The Design-Build Approach

John Cannon Homes specializes in the design-build approach to home building, which brings together professional design and construction expertise to create one harmonious environment. They handle both the design and construction of your home providing a continuity of service that saves time and money, and makes you a partner in the design of your dream home.

As a team, they develop a preliminary floor plan, drawn to your specifications for square footage, number of rooms, and desired features. Then, working with you on the details adding space here or rearranging a room there—until they have on paper exactly what you have in mind.

For sheer beauty and magnificence, John Cannon homes stand apart form the rest. Whether situated in an upscale, master-planned community or nestled in a secluded island paradise, traditional or contemporary, the result is always dazzling!

"We build dream homes. That's what we do, and we don't take our task lightly. Our clients have worked hard to get to where they are, and they deserve the very best" —John and Phillipa Cannon.

Homes by John Cannon are noted for their overall harmony because every element was conceived with the entire home in mind. The design-build approach allows for a seamless design and construction process, providing you with the convenience and consistency of working with a single firm from start to finish.

The John Cannon Homes team consists of the most talented people in their fields-from the sales representatives who greet you at their model homes to the in-house architectural designers, draftsmen, artisans, and trusted subcontractors and suppliers whose mission is to maintain the highest standards in quality, and ensure an exceptional home-building experience for you.

At John Cannon Homes, they never forget that your home is the center of your life—a place to build memories, raise a family, entertain friends, and celebrate life. They are committed to making sure they do it right. The entire John Cannon Homes team aspires to fulfill your dream, and make your home-building experience rewarding and enjoyable. It's your vision. It's their privilege to make it happen.

Those interested in learning more about John Cannon Homes, are encouraged to visit their comprehensive website.

(clockwise from left) John Cannon Homes bedrooms are meant to be as luxurious as they are functional, with connecting baths and spacious walk-in closets, to guest rooms that offer their own sense of privacy.

John Cannon Homes offers the classic, open floor plans that have come to define Florida living, with most living rooms flowing into patios and pool areas.

An extension of the living area, dining rooms expand the main gallery of your home, creating an open, welcome feeling. John Cannon Homes gives special attention to ensure that elegance and style remain in all the details.

Fully equipped islands, commercial-style appliances, and innovative refrigerators that resemble custom-designed cabinetry are just a sampling of how John Cannon Homes creates the perfect balance between form and function.

SERBIN PRINTING

ESTABLISHED 1971 **www.serbinprinting.com**

Browse the gift shops of our local art museum, aquarium, botanical gardens or planetarium and you're likely to get a colorful eyeful of the work produced by Serbin Printing. In addition to the art prints and gift books produced for these attractions, Serbin Printing provides brochures, flyers, catalogs, magazines, and point of purchase materials for a vast array of local, national and international clientele.

Established in 1971, founder Jack Serbin along with his wife Donna opened their first location at the corner of Orange Avenue & Dolphin Street in downtown Sarasota. Things have come a long way since starting with a small duplicator, camera and hand cutter. Later that year their son Mark became a partner in the family business helping to create one of the most successful commercial printing and publishing companies on the Gulf Coast.

Adding an impressive array of equipment over the years, Serbin Printing now offers sophisticated, high-speed large and small format offset printing, digital on-demand printing, full graphic arts and pre-press services. Along with a comprehensive bindery, finishing operation and a full service mailing department, Serbin Printing offers a world of printing solutions for every business. Today located in a beautiful 24,000 square foot facility on North Washington Boulevard in downtown Sarasota, Serbin Printing employs over 45 outstanding craftsmen over two shifts, six days a week.

"The key to our success is our professional and talented staff, our willingness to react to changes in our industry, giving our customers the options they need and our consistent level of high quality work at competitive prices" said Mark Serbin, President. "Our dedication to our customers through customer service, meeting deadlines, producing premium quality work and a commitment to our community are the benchmarks of our success."

GRAVITYFREE

ESTABLISHED 1997 www.gravityfree.com

GravityFree, "The Smart Business Web Agency," has been developing award-winning websites and Internet-based applications for local Sarasota area businesses and nationally recognized entities since 1997. The company mission is to provide accessible Web solutions that meet the clients' strategic objectives.

With clients ranging in size and industry, GravityFree has been able to provide successful Web solutions based on an in-depth understanding of their clients' business goals and Internet technologies. Their approach focuses on results rather than just having a "cool looking" website. From professional graphic design and user-centric functionality to website marketing and analytics, Sarasota's top business organizations have looked to GravityFree as their strategic online partner.

What sets GravityFree apart from other Web developers is its comprehensive approach. They have a team of experts, each highly specialized, who work symbiotically to create the best end-to-end Web solutions for the growing demands of the marketplace and the competitive landscape of the Internet.

In the spring of 2007, GravityFree acquired the Gulf Coast of Florida's most successful Internet marketing firm to incorporate an Internet marketing division at GravityFree. The purpose of this division is to utilize Web marketing strategies and tools to optimize their clients' presence on the Web and deliver better, measurable results. In doing so, they've focused on both "traditional" methods like search engine optimization, pay-per-click advertising, and contextual ad placement, as well as the industry indoctrinated "Web 2.0" practices like the use of blogs, podcasting, video uploading, and other types of user-generated content.

Another unique aspect of GravityFree is that they are the creator of a floral software application called FlowerManager™, which has changed the way flowers and gifts are bought and sold in this country. The nation's largest florists in all major markets around the country, including the Pentagon's flower shop in Washington, DC, are using this technology to sell more flowers, increase customer service and run their shops more effectively.

The values intrinsic to the success of GravityFree include offering the highest quality products and services, empowering their clients, keeping their employees challenged and fulfilled, contributing to the community and supporting their industry on an ongoing basis. These are what has made GravityFree a community mainstay for the past decade and has them poised to lead Sarasota into the future of Web design and Internet marketing.

Office buildings are available for all size businesses and organizations.

the cooperation of the Sarasota Association of Realtors, Commercial and Investment Division, it is updated regularly. The EDC, upon request, will provide built-to-suit quotations based on specific requirements and specifications through its close working relationships with area developers and builders.

Sarasota Means Action Response Team (S.M.A.R.T.) helps expedite site, development and construction permits to approval in 25 working days once all the appropriate paper work has been filed.

An Impact Fee Mitigation Program can eliminate road impact fees for a business relocating or expanding within the county if it is deemed to offer a significant benefit to the local economy.

In 2005, the state approved a boundary expansion of the City of Sarasota and Sarasota County's Enterprise Zone, bringing the total area to approximately 2 square miles. Businesses located within the zone may quality for various tax credits, refunds and exemptions.

The EDC of Sarasota County, in cooperation with the area's government, local municipalities and other significant organizations, has established the Business Express HOTLINE. Area businesses can get assistance in any issue involving the local, state or federal government, from permitting, zoning, regulatory to financial, labor, infrastructure or technical matters. Any calls to the Business HOTLINE receive preliminary assistance within 24 hours.

As one of the most pro-business states in the nation, Florida ranks third in Pollina Corporate Real Estate's Top 10 Pro Business States study. The ranking is based on 28 measurements that included taxes, human resources, right-to-work legislation, energy costs and job growth.

Florida's low corporate income tax rate—5.5 percent of a company's net income in the state—is one of the lowest in the nation. In addition, the state also offers a variety of incentives for businesses operating here, including utility tax credits, tax exemptions for new and expanding businesses, Targeted Jobs Tax Credits (TJTX), qualified Targeted Industry Tax Refunds, Industrial Revenue Bonds, Enterprise Bonds and Technology Transfer Opportunities, to name a few.

There are financial support programs available both through the public and private sectors. Some state and federal programs are designed to provide

W.G. MILLS, INC.

ESTABLISHED 1972 **www.wgmills.com**

Work Hard//Build Right®—
This is the tenet of Sarasota-
based W.G. Mills, Inc.

Construction Excellence based on dedication and total commitment to the success of every project the company undertakes has made W.G. Mills, Inc. one of Florida's largest privately-held General Contracting and Construction Management firms.

As a company, W.G. Mills, Inc. has grown continuously over the past 35 years, expanding to six offices strategically located throughout the state and employing a staff of 225 who work together to annually complete volume in excess of $324 million. This success can be attributed to their "TEAM Approach" to construction delivery and to the quality people who constitute the structure of the company. The firm's financial stability is evidenced by their bonding capacity in excess of $400 million.

W.G. Mills, Inc. maintains a high visibility throughout Florida with offices located in Jacksonville, Palm Beach Gardens, Kissimmee, Clearwater, Fort Myers as well as their corporate headquarters in Sarasota, with an impressive $2.4 billion dollar portfolio of completed projects.

Commitment to customer satisfaction and quality has remained constant since the company's founding in 1972. Under the leadership of senior principals Walter Mills, CEO, Lem Sharp III, President, and Tim Hensey, Executive Vice President, W.G. Mills, Inc. brings unrivaled construction experience combined with a motivated and professional staff that is without equal in the industry. The firm prides itself on completing projects within budget and under strict time requirements while simultaneously maintaining rigorous quality standards. The ability to consistently master

these challenges translates into a repeat client following.

One of the firm's core values is the principle that the construction process is a team effort involving multiple team members, including Owner, Architect, Engineer, Interior Designer, and Construction Manager. W.G. Mills, Inc. has the experience and leadership required to foster effective communication, cooperation, and coordination between all team members involved in a construction project. The staff knows how to mobilize as a team, to build on its strengths, and to complement the abilities of all involved to reach the common goal of delivering a quality project on time and on budget.

While looking back proudly on 35 years of success in Florida, a rare achievement in a fiercely competitive industry, the principals at W.G. Mills, Inc. are committed to taking the company to the next level of Construction Excellence with integrity, reliability and commitment.

funding to purchase fixed assets at below market rates. Others focus on small businesses, seeking to get companies started and help them grow.

GulfCoast Business Finance, Inc., a private, nonprofit organization in St. Petersburg, assists Florida businesses in securing long-term, fixed interest rate Small Business Administration (SBA) funding for capital expansion projects.

The EDC has a website, businessfundingresource.com, that identifies available capital and financing sources for existing businesses and start-up companies. It can also arrange for businesses to talk with representatives of the Southwest Florida Regional Development Corporation, which can assist with Small Business Administration 504 Loan Programs.

Businesses in Florida may also qualify for Quick Response Training Grants for their employees. Since 1993, Quick Response has provided customized training for more than 100,000 employees for more than 300 businesses throughout the state. Companies obviously like the way we do business. In 2007, *Inc.* magazine put Sarasota-Bradenton-Venice No. 8 on a list of 393 "boomtowns," and No. 3 among midsize cities. All indicators bode well for the area's growth and prosperity.

finance &
professions

finance &
professions

WHILE SARASOTA RETAINS SOME OF THE QUALITIES of a small town, where business can be conducted on a handshake, it is as sophisticated as any big city when it comes to finances. Large national banks and investment firms exist side by side with local financial institutions, and there are a wide variety of resources available for both residents and businesses.

There are also creative, visionary leaders in a number of financial arenas. Commercial real estate brokers, for example, have been involved in some of the region's landmark real estate deals. In one instance, the purchase of rundown bungalows in Towles Court and securing special zoning provisions from the city were instrumental in turning it into a trendy artists' colony. They also put together the tricky financing for The Ritz-Carlton, Sarasota, the first hotel/condo combination in the U.S.

The banking and real estate professions are well represented in Sarasota's downtown.

As one of Florida's leading business centers, the Gulf Coast area has attracted some of the largest banks in the nation—Bank of America, Wachovia, SunTrust, Washington Mutual and JPMorgan Chase—with Bank of America holding the greatest single market share in the Sarasota-Manatee county area. Regions, which recently merged with AmSouth, is aggressively expanding into the area.

There is also a substantial number of independent community banks throughout the two counties. In 2006, the Sarasota-Bradenton-Venice market had 45 banks with 298 offices. Their combined total of $16.5 billion in deposits, according to the FDIC, represented the fifth largest market share in Florida.

The community bank movement began in the late 1990s when the mega banks merged across Florida, creating a niche for more personalized banking. Most of the new banks were started by experienced professionals from larger banking institutions, and all were well connected to the community. As they achieved success, some were purchased by larger banks seeking to expand into the local market, making community banks a good business and investment opportunity as well. This led to

another wave of startups. In 2004, state regulators received more bank applications than any other time since 1998.

As the local market and economy grows, banks such as The Bank of Commerce, LandMark Bank, Horizon, Freedom, First America and Insignia Bank continue to flourish. With their intimate knowledge of the community, they serve checking and savings account holders who like a personal touch. They also provide construction loans for local real estate development, fund business expansion, finance retail inventories, and support small business startups.

The enactment of the Financial Service Modernization Act in 1999 allowed banks to open other fee-earning lines of business. As a result, they now compete with mortgage companies, investment firms and brokerage houses throughout the region. The large real estate market, however, continues to support a wide variety of small and large mortgage and brokerage firms.

At the same time, Sarasota County's high concentration of wealthy residents ensures that other national financial institutions beside banks have a significant presence here. Merrill Lynch, one of the world's leading financial management and advisory companies, and A.G. Edwards

WINDOM MORTGAGE SERVICES, INC.

ESTABLISHED 1999 www.windommortgageservices.com

Exceptional Service You Deserve

Windom Mortgage Services Inc. is focused on providing customers with choice, convenience, and expertise. Whether you are looking for a residential or commercial property loan, you're not just receiving years of experience and access to a wide variety of lenders, but a genuine piece of Sarasota.

The owner, Bob Windom, is a life long resident of Sarasota. His family has played an active role here for three generations. His grandfather was the first city manager and his father had a prominent medical practice in town while later becoming the US Assistant Secretary for Health in the Reagan administration.

Being involved in the community is second nature to Windom. He was elected to the Sarasota County Hospital Board when he was 24 years old and became president of the Sarasota Jaycees. He sat on the board of United Way and currently the Berlin Branch YMCA Board. He also is a former president of the Sarasota Executive Network and the Florida Federation of Young Republicans.

With Windom Mortgage Services, home buyers who are relocating or just entering the market are in good hands. The same goes for clients opting to refinance an existing mortgage, wanting to take out

a home equity loan, planning to invest in real estate or needing a construction loan.

Working relationships with a wide variety of lenders allows the company to offer wholesale pricing as well as providing an extensive array of choices and affordable loans. Those individuals and families with strong credit profiles benefit from these relationships, while other clients who are self-employed can opt for no income, no asset verification loans. Help is also available for credit injured borrowers.

Windom Mortgage Services is a hands-on mortgage brokerage

firm. Bob Windom himself visits clients in their homes and offices, and he is easy to reach. "My name is attached to the company," he says. "When clients call, they talk to me."

The approach has paid off. Word of mouth is strong, and the company enjoys a steady repeat business. "Referrals are a stamp of approval that we did a good job," Windom explains. For someone who cares about his clients and the future of the community, this is important. "We are established here...trusted here," he says. "We are here to stay."

INSIGNIA BANK

ESTABLISHED 2006 **www.insigniabank.com**

"Banking wherever and whenever you need"

A community is defined by its people. So is its bank. Insignia Bank is a very different kind of bank; one that has the financial strength to combine sophisticated banking with personalized service, expertly tailored for you. The *Insignia style* of banking is delivered in a unique environment that has no peer. Think about it as banking wherever and whenever you need. Sound like your kind of bank? Then welcome to Insignia Bank.

From the very start they have been different. Insignia Bank had the largest private capital campaign ever for a start-up bank in Sarasota history; raising over $25 million in capital in less than six weeks. And since capital is one of the key

measurements of safety, as an Insignia client, you are assured of banking with one of the best.

Insignia Bank offers all the latest technology and provides you key benefits such as free ATM usage anywhere nationwide and free online banking, allowing you to access and manage your money wherever you are, all without coming to the bank.

"When wherever, whenever feels like home"

However, when you do have the occasion to come into one of the Insignia Bank offices, you immediately notice the differences. You feel like you are home. From the outgoing employees who greet you, to the fresh-baked cookies and coffee you are offered, to the flat screen televisions, to the overall design

of the bank—you feel as though you are at a grand estate, and one that you just happen to own.

The unique differences are expressed everywhere—in their very non-traditional boardroom at the main office in Sarasota, for example, you discover details such as flat screen TVs, authentic Venetian plaster, and even a living room! And keeping true to the Florida heritage, you ascend to the second story of the building, where two outdoor terraces allow you to do your banking "al fresco..." a unique kind of banking, tailored to you.

To experience this "wherever, whenever" Insignia style of banking, new and existing clients have convenient office locations to stop by or can access these privileges by visiting Insignia Bank's comprehensive website.

INTERSHOW

ESTABLISHED 1978 **www.moneyshow.com**

InterShow, headquartered in Sarasota, Florida, is the world's leading producer of investment trade shows and cruises and has been producing live forums of communication for people with a passion for investing since 1978. Prompted by their own needs, founders Charles and Kim Githler, set out to create interactive educational opportunities that offered informative exchanges and insights of the quality that they themselves were seeking.

Over time these seminars developed into The Money Show, which pioneered a unique concept and business model that has proven to be a resounding success nationally. Responding to world trends and international markets, they expanded the model to the global arena with their production of The World Money Show. Following the unprecedented success of these events, InterShow expanded to address the needs of more specialized industry segments such as The Traders Expo, The Financial Advisor

Symposium, and The Forex Trading Expo. Cruise seminars produced by InterShow are exclusive and luxurious events that focus not only on investing, but also on health, intellectual stimulation, and principles of business success across a variety of industries.

In 2007, InterShow launched MoneyShow.com—a virtual InterShow event that offers investors, traders, and financial advisors 24/7 multi-media access to investment and trading education and resources direct from industry experts.

Designed as an educational destination for each audience, MoneyShow.com is broken into three virtual channels to provide easy access to the commentary and recommendations of Wall Street and trading experts specifically for investors, traders, and financial advisors. MoneyShow.com features MarketResource, the first comprehensive search engine in the financial services industry where users can search 1,000+

financial service companies, 1,500+ InterShow speakers, and more than 10,000 publicly traded companies by ticker symbol, to discover advice, education, recommendations, and tools from Wall Street experts and financial services companies.

MoneyShow.com also features Top Pros' Top Picks, a section providing daily articles of digested commentary and specific stock picks from leading industry experts, and Gurus' Views & Strategies, which features market commentary from top investment advisers; both are distributed via weekly and daily e-mails. Users of the site will also discover Live and On-Demand Webcasts: 5, 15, 45 and 90 minute webcasts from the experts giving workshops and panels at InterShow events. During live webcasts users can even ask questions of the speakers through an online Q&A tool. For members who are looking for an in-depth education, MoneyShow.com has created the MoneyShow University, the only online university offering video courses where members can learn from leading financial experts through university style multi-media courses in 100, 200, and 300 levels.

Through the development of MoneyShow.com, InterShow will extend its reach beyond conference attendees to the entire globe to further its mission to stimulate business, foster education, and raise the level of awareness of both investors and providers creating a more conscious marketplace.

MERRILL LYNCH

ESTABLISHED 1915 **www.ml.com**

For nearly 100 years, Merrill Lynch has built a tradition of trust by continually anticipating the changing needs of our clients and providing them with the highest level of service. Financial Advisors consider every aspect of a client's financial life, going beyond financial solutions to offer customized wealth management advice, products and services that help our clients achieve their goals and dreams.

Total Merrill_{SM}...
Merrill Lynch offers a comprehensive platform of products and services that includes everything from investments to mortgages, banking services, cash management and credit cards, trust and generational planning, consumer and small business lending, and retirement services. Total Merrill_{SM} captures in a single phrase what their Financial Advisors do every day—provide clients with a lifetime of solutions based on their total financial picture. Solutions that go well beyond investments. In doing so, Merrill Lynch's Financial Advisors become essential partners to clients; creating opportunities, anticipating needs and helping turn visions into reality, ultimately helping them achieve the lives they've always wanted.

Resources at Work For You...
Financial Advisors are at the center of clients' financial lives, and provide the resources to help them deliver a superior level of service. The Sarasota Complex of Merrill Lynch has served the financial needs of Sarasota and surrounding communities for more than 50 years, with over 100 Financial Advisors, and offices in Sarasota, Bradenton, Venice, Punta Gorda, and Sebring.

and American Express all have offices here offering counsel to local investors. Over the past 20 years, Raymond James in St. Petersburg has grown from a community bank to a nationwide, diversified financial service company and is well represented throughout the Gulf Coast region. There are also a number of smaller, independent financial firms throughout the two-county area that provide asset management and investment advice.

Other finance related companies include InterShow, which has its headquarters in Sarasota. As the world's leading producer of investment trade shows, it developed a highly successful program—The Money Show. Since 1978, it has connected tens of thousands of individual investors with business professionals and expert speakers in the investment arena.

In addition, Ruden McClosky, one of Florida's largest and fastest growing law firms, has offices in Sarasota and St. Petersburg, providing a full range of legal services and business solutions to local companies and high wealth clients.

To continue to encourage a thriving area business climate, the EDC of Sarasota County has partnered with local financial institutions and existing local and regional angel investor networks to assess the full range of capital available for new and established companies. The EDC also maintains a website, www.businessfundingresource. com, where it collects relevant information about all the financial resources available for starting a new business or expanding an existing venture, including angel and venture capital, bank and bond financing, grants, import/export financing and public offerings.

A new EDC strategy focuses on tapping the existing wealth in the community for startup and expansion business financing and to continue to create a solid foundation for economic growth throughout the county. An important aspect of this strategy includes taking into account the overall profile, as population growth affects all industries and economic aspects of a community.

Thus, it is significant that the largest group in Sarasota County is in the 34 to 54 age range. This group includes the leaders and emerging leaders in business and community affairs, who are motivated to build a strong economy for the future. Their immediate concerns are varied, depending on which part of the spectrum they occupy. There is an active Young

Professionals Group, for example, which is part of The Greater Sarasota Chamber of Commerce. The organization provides opportunities for its members to network and gain leadership experience and training, as well as take part in making decisions on important topics that affect the community.

The second largest group is 65 to 79 year olds, a remarkably active group of retirees and semi-retired individuals. Many of them continue to offer their expertise and advice on business and community matters, participate on the board of numerous non-profit organizations, and take advantage of the area's many artistic, cultural and recreational activities. They make up a substantial number of the area's dedicated volunteers and social movers and shakers who support a wide variety of businesses, non-profit agencies and charity organizations.

The fact that residents under the age of 17 years comprise the third largest group bodes well for the future of the county. They are growing up with the benefit of superior educational opportunities, and many will make their mark in the region's professions and industries, continuing to spur growth and ensuring that business and technology development will remain cutting edge and up-to-date.

Next in line are the 55 to 64 year olds, a dynamic, forward-looking group. Some in this group, having taken early retirement, are embarking on their second or third career and starting new businesses. Others are still pursuing their professions or participating in running companies. They are active in expanding the community's assets, managing ongoing growth, and contributing to the area's future prosperity and success.

Close on their heels in numbers are the 18 to 34 year olds, many of whom are entering the area's diverse professions, businesses and industries for the first time. Eager to test themselves and apply what they have learned, they also represent the largest sector of workers who take advantage of the many continuing education opportunities available throughout the area.

Finally, there is a substantial group of retirees age 80 years and older. Many of them remain active and involved in issues that concern the community. A surprising number continue to act as volunteers, play golf, attend theater and musical performances, and take full advantage of all the great lifestyle opportunities the area has to offer.

RUDEN McCLOSKY

ESTABLISHED 1959 **www.ruden.com**

Local Strength, Statewide Resources

With 200 attorneys in a full range of practice areas, Ruden McClosky is considered to be one of the largest and most prominent law firms in Florida. Since its founding in 1959, the firm has grown to serve clients throughout the state and internationally from its ten Florida offices and one office in Caracas, Venezuela. Offering both strength, through its statewide network of legal resources, and knowledge of the Sarasota/Manatee area, the attorneys of the Sarasota office of Ruden McClosky have been serving our community's legal needs for over 30 years.

Ruden McClosky serves businesses, governments, not-for-profit organizations and high wealth individuals. Their attorneys share a commitment to providing quality legal counsel with integrity and professionalism. The firm's practice groups offer focused legal counsel in banking and finance, bankruptcy, community association, construction, corporate, environmental, governmental relations, healthcare, immigration, intellectual property, international, labor and employment, land use and zoning, civil and criminal litigation, natural resources, real estate, tax, and trusts and estates. The breadth and depth of Ruden McClosky's practice areas position the Sarasota attorneys to be able to fulfill their clients' specific and unique legal needs. Regionally, the firm has played a key role in helping to define the face of Sarasota County through its involvement in the area's biggest real estate transactions; local governmental issues relating to land use, environment, and acquisitions; and other significant matters in both the public and private sectors.

The attorneys of the Sarasota office have made a positive impact on our community as well through their many community contributions. Through the donation of countless hours to a number of local charitable and civic organizations, the firm has made a long-term commitment to enhancing the overall health and wellbeing of the Sarasota community.

As an employer, Ruden McClosky attracts top graduates of major law schools from around the state and nation to the Sarasota area. The firm's diverse workforce of attorneys and staff cross racial, gender and ethnic lines to offer clients the benefit of working with top tier professionals who are reflective of today's society.

The lawyers of Ruden McClosky, left to right: Tom Dart, Louis Ursini, Nicholas Gladding, Barry Spivey, Tami Conetta, Karen Morinelli, Ronald Shapo, Bo Kim, Cynthia Fallon, Robert Gill, Laura Bauman, David Boyette, Jason Gaskill and John Dart

RAYMOND JAMES® & ASSOCIATES, INC.

ESTABLISHED 1976 WWW.RAYMONDJAMES.COM/SARASOTA

Front Row: Regina Sakezles, WMS™, AAMS™, Manager. Middle Row: Michael Tutcher, MBA, CLU™, CHFC™, REBC™; Lyn Rogers, WMS™, Retirement Plan Consultant. Back Row: Michael Scrementi, WMS™; Allan Gottesman, WMS™, Retirement Plan Consultant; Richard Crawford, CFP™. Not pictured: John Meyers, WMS™.

Individual Solutions from Independent Advisors

Discover the professionals at the downtown Sarasota branch of Raymond James & Associates, Inc. They pride themselves on giving uncompromising attention to your needs. Whether your goals involve retirement planning, education planning, or estate planning, Raymond James offers a wealth of resources and solutions to help ensure your goals are met.

Raymond James financial advisors have over 135 years of industry experience. Among the industry designations and advanced degrees their advisors hold are: Certified Financial Planner, Chartered Life Underwriter, Chartered Financial Consultant, Master of Business Administration,

Registered Employee Benefits Consultant, Wealth Management Specialist, Legacy Planner, Retirement Plan Consultant, Chartered Mutual Fund Counselor, Chartered Retirement Planning Counselor, and Accredited Asset Management Specialist.

Community involvement is very important to the firm. Some of the community organizations they support include: Manatee Community College Foundation, Investment Policy Committee of Manatee Community College, Sarasota County Animal Services, Fraternal Order of Eagles, Boys & Girls Clubs of Sarasota County, The Greater Sarasota Chamber of Commerce, Sarasota School Superintendent's Business Advisory Committee, Endowment Committee for St. Wilfred Episcopal Church, South County

YMCA, Asolo Repertory Theatre for the Performing Arts, City of North Port Chamber of Commerce—Government Affairs and Economic Development, Lakewood Ranch High School Band Booster Association, Ducks Unlimited, Manatee County Sheriffs Department, Sarasota Harley Owners Group, Historic Spanish Point, Advisory Council of the Metropolitan Planning Organization, as well as having several Rotarians in the office.

Raymond James provides direct access to all the services the financial industry has to offer. We can help you grow your portfolio with managed accounts of stocks and bonds, acquire initial public offerings, or protect your assets with a wide array of protection products and comprehensive financial planning. For every great relationship, there's one place from which it all begins—Raymond James.

Their Financial Advisors and industry experts are great sources of knowledge, and they encourage you to take advantage of their services. They are here to help you simplify your life.

Raymond James is proud to be located in the very heart of downtown Sarasota where its unique culture, architecture, and restaurants can be appreciated. The next time you are near the Sarasota City Center, drop in and say hello. They would love to meet you!

REGIONS

ESTABLISHED 1854 **www.regions.com**

Regions' brand promise, "It's time to expect more", reflects the pledge to make Regions a bank that's easy to do business with and reflects the commitment to be more than just a bank. Regions Bank is not just in the business of banking; Regions is in the business of life.

Regions Bank selected a pyramid as the centerpiece of the logo because of its unique structure, and perhaps more importantly, because each side is of equal length, which symbolizes the equal attention Regions devotes to customers, associates and the community.

The Regions Pyramid is also divided by five rays, which reflect the basic values: 1) put people first; 2) do what is right; 3) focus on your customer; 4) reach higher; and 5) enjoy life.

The bicycle in Regions' logo, billboards and other marketing materials, represents the kind of experience customers want from Regions. It reminds people of reliability, simplicity, less complication and more enjoyment. It also is a symbol that the customer experience is a journey—not a destination.

The banking experience should be as simple as riding a bike. Regions is committed to giving customers the quality services and products they need to manage their personal and business finances and the easier, more enjoyable experience they want. It's time to expect more.

Regions Financial Corporation is a member of the S&P 100 Index and *Forbes Magazine's* "Platinum 400" list of America's best big companies. With nearly

$140 billion in assets, Regions is one of the nation's largest full-service providers of consumer and commercial banking, trust, securities brokerage, mortgage and insurance products and services. Regions serves customers in 16 states across the South, Midwest and Texas, and through its subsidiary,

Regions Bank, operates some 1,900 AmSouth and Regions banking offices and more than 2,400 ATMs. Its investment and securities brokerage trust and asset management division, Morgan Keegan & Company Inc., provides services from more than 400 offices.

More information about Regions and its full line of products and services can be found on their website.

vistas for
tomorrow

vistas for tomorrow

IN 1885, WHEN A HANDFUL OF SCOTTISH COLONISTS first arrived on the shores of Sarasota, the town and seacoast settlements to the south were just sleepy fishing villages. A few hearty pioneers farmed and raised cattle farther inland. The rest of the county was largely unexplored, a wilderness inhabited by bobcat, armadillos and alligators. A mere 125 years later, a network of roads and highways would crisscross the county to connect cities and communities.

Tourists and year-round residents flock to Sarasota to bask in the sunshine on its world famous beaches, enjoy a wealth of recreational opportunities, and partake of a flourishing art and cultural scene. Business and manufacturing are thriving as well, with companies relocating here to take advantage of the area's favorable business climate. Sarasota and environs is rapidly becoming one of the leading 21st century communities.

As Florida's 14th most populous county, the Sarasota area continues to grow and is expected to see an increase of more than 170,000 residents over the next 25 years, expanding the population to 532,000.

Such unprecedented growth has been driving recent development and will continue to require expansion of residential communities driven by the need to keep pace with this growth.

The year 2007 was a banner year for downtown Sarasota real estate development, with two major mixed-use projects getting underway. The Quay on U.S. 41 just north of the bay was demolished to make way for a $1 billion luxury venture, to be called Sarasota Bayside. It will have four 14-story towers, 700 high-end condominiums, hotels, retail outlets and restaurants.

At the same time, the Pineapple Square project, a $200 million conglomeration of condos, parking spaces and upscale shops got its start in the heart of the city.

Another massive $1 billion project along U.S. 41 is in the planning stages. The Procenium, slated for a six-acre tract across from Sarasota Bayside, will be anchored by a Waldorf-Astoria hotel with 225 rooms and 35,000 square feet of meeting space. The development also includes a new 800-seat theater, designed for a wide variety of entertainment such as concerts, dance and film. But the main attraction will be small Broadway and off-Broadway touring productions presented by Nederlander Worldwide Entertainment, which owns several theaters in New York. Sarasota's commitment to the arts continues unabated in other ways as well.

After more than four years of citizen's workshops, public hearings and advice from consultants, the Sarasota City Commission recently passed a "concept plan" for a Cultural Park. The 42-acre area by the bay along U.S. 41, bordered by the Boulevard of the Arts and 10th Street, will include the Van Wezel Performing Arts Hall, G.WIZ Hands-On Science Museum, the Florida West Coast Symphony, a sculpture garden and a fishing pier. Existing and new arts venues will be connected by tree-covered walkways and scenic landscaping.

Innovation 41, the master plan designed to integrate the cultural and educational institutions along the U.S. 41 corridor from the Sarasota-Bradenton International Airport to downtown Sarasota will give that area a unique, unified character and create an exciting gateway to the region. These are busy times throughout the county as well in anticipation of greater need for residential facilities, retail outlets and office space.

For example, Fruitville Road near I-75 is undergoing construction. Anchored by a Lowe's Home Improvement store, there will be space for a number of new businesses and restaurants.

Ringling Bridge connecting downtown Sarasota to Lido Beach.

University Town Center, an open-air collection of shops and restaurants located just west of I-75 on University Parkway, was recently purchased by Benderson Development Company. Plans for expansion include a massive mixed-use project of 1.5 million square feet of upscale retail space, three hotels, office buildings, a movie theater and 1,750 residences.

Based on the success of Lakewood Ranch creating a master-planned community, several other large scale residential developments are occurring in the southern part of the county. Thomas Ranch in North Port and Venice plans to build at least 15,000 new homes along with shops, parks and other amenities.

In the education arena, many positive changes are taking place. With New College and USF Sarasota-Manatee now located on separate campuses, both institutions will be able to develop on their own, creating new programs and expanding to meet the need of a 21st century education.

The USF Sarasota-Manatee Leadership Council, which advises the university on creating new programs that serve the area's business and manufacturing needs, will continue to encourage the development of a skilled labor force that can meet the challenges of the new global market.

The Ringling College of Art and Design has just added a number of new majors and continues to plan for major physical expansion. The new programs and facilities will position the school at the cutting edge of 21st century art education and cement its position as one of the leading art and design schools in the world. The Sarasota County School District is looking to forge new programs to further the area's superior education, including NeXt Generation Learning, an ambitious five-year plan seeking to explore ways to better prepare students for college and beyond. As part of the Florida High Tech Corridor, the Sarasota-Manatee area will continue to attract cutting edge business and manufacturing companies.

To meet their needs, there are plans for further commerce park development throughout the county, especially in new emerging communities in Lakewood Ranch, north Venice and North Port.

At the same time, the EDC of Sarasota County and its counterpart in Manatee County are actively pursuing ways of attracting new companies, while supporting established businesses in the area. To that end, it has developed grassroots cluster groups—networks of like businesses and the suppliers and educational institutions that serve those businesses. The initiative also addresses the need to create partnerships both locally and regionally to ensure a sustainable economy and environment.

Emerging clusters that have already received considerable attention include Life & Environmental Services, Specialty Manufacturing, Creative Services and Business Climate Work Group. Activities have included organizing national conferences, offering tours for middle and high school students of local manufacturing facilities and technical schools, and producing directories and databases to serve job seekers and employers.

The Life & Environmental Science Cluster, for example, focuses on sustainable and environmentally sound growth. To that end, the EDC organized a symposium on "Natural Capitalism," a progressive approach to building wealth, creating a healthy environment and enhancing quality of life. In Creative Services, a Web-based directory of film-related services available in Sarasota County is intended to attract film and video production.

In the future, the growing cluster of area businesses focusing on commercial applications in the fields of medicine, environmental management, horticulture and aquaculture is likely to continue expanding.

Adapting to the change in population demographics and business diversity, as well as developing our cultural venues, education networks, and medical and social services will require increasing awareness and partnerships of all public and private sectors.

Preparing to manage the growth while preserving our natural beauty and resources is an ongoing challenge for all municipal and county governmental organizations.

The Downtown Master Plan 2020 for the City of Sarasota, developed by famed architect and urban theorist Andres Duany, is one such effort to look ahead and manage the ongoing expansion while preserving Sarasota's history.

An active program to purchase tracts of land for parks and preservation of pristine areas throughout the county seeks to ensure that the natural beauty of the area will be enjoyed by generations to come.

The ongoing debates between slow-growth advocates and supporters of more rapid development go to the heart of how to best create sustainable economic development, while preserving Sarasota's history, charm and amenities — all things that make the area so attractive to residents, visitors, business and corporations.

We invite you to become part of our future and share the extraordinary experience of living and working in a county whose natural beauty, historical charm, business and leisure resources and opportunities make for an unrivaled quality of life.

SARASOTA AREA MAP

0   Scale in Miles   5

© 2008 The Map Group, Inc.

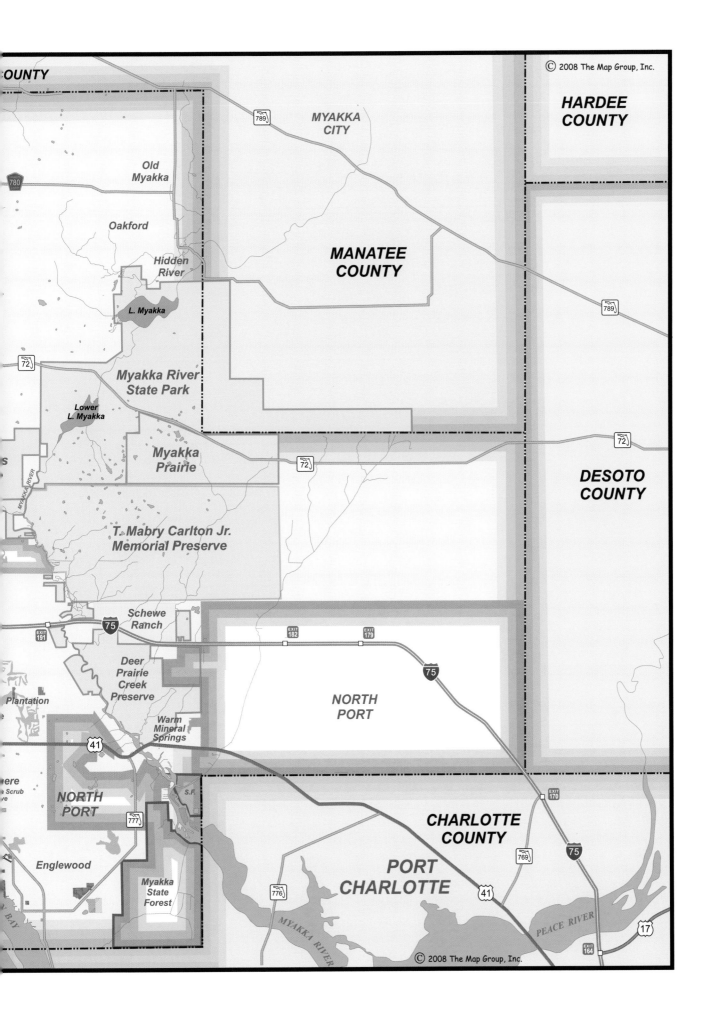

HARDEE COUNTY

OUNTY

Old Myakka

Oakford

Hidden River

L. Myakka

789

MYAKKA CITY

MANATEE COUNTY

780

72

Myakka River State Park

Lower L. Myakka

789

72

Myakka Prairie

72

DESOTO COUNTY

T. Mabry Carlton Jr. Memorial Preserve

75

Schewe Ranch

EXIT 191

EXIT 182

EXIT 179

75

NORTH PORT

Deer Prairie Creek Preserve

Plantation

Warm Mineral Springs

41

EXIT 170

CHARLOTTE COUNTY

NORTH PORT

ere a Scrub ve

777

Englewood

Myakka State Forest

S.F.

PORT CHARLOTTE

776

769

75

41

MYAKKA RIVER

PEACE RIVER

17

EXIT 164

205

index

patron index

references

Books and Publications

Board, Prudy Taylor and Colcord, Esther B., *Venice through the Years: A Pictorial History*, The Dionning Company/Publishers, Virginia Beach, VA, 1995.

Cortes, Josephine O., *The History of Early Englewood: From the Newspaper Columns of Josephine O. Cortes*, Funcoast Publishing Co., Punta Gorda, FL, 1976.

Dickenman, Joan Berry, *The Homesteaders: Early Settlers of Nokomis and Laurel*, St. Petersburg, FL, 1987.

Elder, Amy A., *Sarasota*, Arcadia Publishing, Charleston, SC, 2003.

Grismer, Karl H., *The Story of Sarasota: The History of the City and County of Sarasota, Florida*, Florida Grower Press, Tampa, FL, 1944.

Matthews, Janet Snyder, *Journey to Centennial*, rev. edition, Pine Level Press, Sarasota, FL, 1997.

Matthews, Janet Snyder, *Venice: Journey from Horse and Chaise*, Pine Level Press, Sarasota, FL 1989.

LaHurd, Jeff, *Quintessential Sarasota: Stories and Pictures from the 1920s to the 1950s*, History Press, Charleston, SC, 2004.

LaHurd, Jeff, edited by Nance Wilke, *Sarasota, Then and Now*, Sarasota Alliance for Historic Preservation, 1994.

LaHurd, Jeff, *Sarasota: A History*, History Press, Charleston, SC, 2006.

Schofield, Arthur C., *Yesterday's Bradenton including Manatee County*, Lindsey Curtis Pub., Bradenton, FL, 1984

Wilpon, Bonnie, *Sarasota and Bradenton Florida*, Arcadia Publishing, Charleston, SC, 1999.

Turner, Paul H. and Turner, Joan Berry, *The Seekers: Pioneer Families of Nokomis and Laurel*, Turner Publications, Laurel, FL, 1979.

Turner, Gregg M., *Venice in the 1920s*, Arcadia Publishing, Charleston, SC, 2000.

Articles and Special Reports

"America's Best Value College," *Princeton Review*, April 24, 2007.

"America's Top 100 Golf Communities," *Travel & Leisure Golf*, January 2007.

"Best Places to Retire Young," *CNN/Money Magazine*, April 17, 2007.

"Boomtowns—2007, *Inc. Magazine*, May 2007.

"Best Cities for Jobs," *Forbes*, February 16, 2007.

Economic Development Corporation of Sarasota County, *Prosperity by Design: Sarasota County Florida Community Profile*, Sarasota, FL 2006-2007 Edition.

Economic Development Corporation of Sarasota County, *A Guide to Doing Business: Sarasota County, Florida*, Sarasota, FL, 2006-2007 Edition.

"On the Beach: Insider's Guide," *Sarasota*, Volume 29, Number 3, 2007.

"10 Best Markets for Small Business," *BizJournals*, July 8, 2007.

"2007 Top Cities for Business Attraction: These Communities Are Literally Magnets for Business," *Expansion Management*, June 19, 2007.

"2007 America's Best Hospitals," *U.S. News & World Report*, August 23, 2007.

"2005 METRO PUBLIC SCHOOLS QUOTIENT: Which Metro Areas Have the Best Public Education Systems?" *Expansion Management*, April 14, 2005.

Websites

Economic Development Corporation of Sarasota County:
http://www.edcsarasotacounty.com

Economic Development Corporation of Bradenton and Manatee County:
http://www.manateeedc.com

Englewood-Cape Haze Chamber of Commerce:
http://www.englewoodchamber.com

Enterprise Florida, Inc.: Sarasota County Profile:
http://www.eflorida.com/profiles/CountyReport.asp?CountyID =14&Display=all

Enterprise Florida, Inc.: Manatee County Profile
http://www.eflorida.com/profiles/County Report.asp?CountyID=65&Display=all

Florida High Tech Corridor:
http://www.floridahightech.com

The Greater Sarasota Chamber of Commerce:
http://www.sarasotachamber.com

History of Sarasota County:
www.scg.co.sarasota.fl.us/Historical resources/history/index.asp

Longboat Key, St Armands Key, Lido Key Chamber of Commerce:
http://www.longboatkeychamber.com

Manatee Chamber of Commerce:
http://www.manateechamber.com

Manatee County Government:
http://www.co.manatee.fl.us

National Civic League's All-American City Award: http://www.ncl.org/aac/past_winners/past_winners.html#06 (2007)

Relocate-America.com:
http://top100.relocate-america.com (2007)

Sarasota County Government:
http://www.scgov.net

Sarasota County School District:
http://www.sarasotacountyschools.net

Sarasota Memorial Health Care System:
www.http://www.smh.com/index.html (2007)

State of Florida: Official Portal:
http://www.myflorida.com

Tampa Bay Partnership:
http://www.tampabay.org

Venice Area Chamber of Commerce:
http://www.venicechamber.com

public art

Chapter 1
Title Unknown, John Ringling
Boulevard, St. Armands Circle

Chapter 2
The One that Got Away,
Sun Circle Park

Chapter 3
Olympic Wannabees, Main Street
& Pineapple Avenue

Chapter 4
Ellipsota, Main Street at Herald-
Tribune Media Group

Chapter 5
Applause, N. Tamiami Trail
at the Van Wezel Performing
Arts Hall

Chapter 6
Discus Thrower, John Ringling
Boulevard, St. Armands Circle

Chapter 7
Exotic 10, Main Street & Palm
Avenue

Chapter 8
Cycle Series, Fruitville Road at
The Greater Sarasota Chamber
of Commerce

Chapter 9
Synergy, Mecca Drive &
Bay Shore Road

Chapter 10
People's Place, Main Street &
Pineapple Avenue

Chapter 11
John Ringling, John Ringling
Boulevard, St. Armands Circle

Chapter 12
Photon II, N. Tamiami Trail
at the Van Wezel Performing
Arts Hall